Advance Praise for *The Mini*

"Dr. McCabe is the most knowledgeable, relatable sports psychologist I have ever come across. He is able to put the science of psychology into common sense and that is exactly what you see in *The MindSide Manifesto*. As an athlete, the urgency to compete is at the core of everything that I do. Dr. McCabe's principles outlined in this book will not only take your game to the next level, but they will take your life to the next level!"

– Haylie McCleney
Professional Softball Player, Team USA, 2016 World Champion

"It's one thing to have dreams, it's another to have the ability to realize them. In *The MindSide Manifesto*, Dr. McCabe explains that you're not born with the ability to face fear and push through self-doubt; it's a skill that is learned and exercised. This is an eye-opening handbook with a practical blueprint on how to break through mental barriers we set up for ourselves and move forward without fear or self-doubt. This is a must read for everyone."

– Trillium Rose
PGA and LPGA Golf Instructor, Head Director of Instruction at Woodmont Country Club in Maryland, Awarded "America's Best Young Teachers" by Golf Digest

"Having known Bhrett for many years, I have seen him produce results over and over again, and now he is sharing his own bank of knowledge and experiences with all in *The MindSide Manifesto*. The Manifesto is a must have framework for any athlete who is striving to get the most out of their practice and play."

– Joe Hallet
Director of Golf Instruction at Vanderbilt Legends Club, Top 50 Golf Instructor by Golf Range Magazine and Golf Magazine Top 100 Instructor

"Dr. McCabe's book introduces a powerful framework for any athlete looking to excel. The focus on "process vs. results" has been mentioned over and over, but this is the first book I have read that provides practical ways to make this a reality. Learning to compete to execute and not just survive is a champion's attitude, and Bhrett gives you a rare insight into how to best develop this winning mindset."

– Dr. Greg Cartin
Sports Psychologist

"*The MindSide Manifesto* is a tremendous read for any athlete, coach, or high performer. Dr. McCabe's story teaches numerous lessons on the impact our psychology has on performance."

– Matt Morse
Performance Coach

"As performance coaches we spend 80% of our programming trying to optimize our athletes performance variables so they can excel when given the opportunity to be great! But what are we doing to help them when the @$%# hits the fan? Dr. McCabe and The MindSide created a complete shift in the way we approach the mental aspect of performance. Instead of putting all of our energy into a potential moment that may never happen, he focuses on how to handle the inevitable. The Greats are remembered by their highlight reels, but the way they handled the hard times, fought through with grit, overcame obstacles, their undeniable spirit and how they routinely delivered when others fail is what truly made them GREAT! This book provides the reader with the skills to pay the bills when everyone else is bouncing checks!"

– Jason Glass
BHK CSCS, Host of the Coach Glass Podcast

THE MINDSIDE MANIFESTO

THE URGENCY TO CREATE A COMPETITIVE MINDSET

Written By

Bhrett McCabe, PhD

60x6 PUBLISHING

BIRMINGHAM, AL

The MindSide Manifesto:
The Urgency to Create a Competitive Mindset

Copyright © 2017 by Bhrett McCabe

606 Publishing

www.themindside.com
orders@themindside.com

FIRST EDITION

Editorial supervision by Gary Perkinson
Design by Hunter Crawford

ISBN 978-0-9982174-0-6

"Successful mindsets do not suddenly appear — they are formed and declared."

– Dr. Bhrett McCabe

Prelude

The challenge of writing this book was to produce something that captured the high-performance mindset found in great athletes, coaches, and business leaders, without producing another book that focused on the traditional natures of sports psychology and motivation, particularly with the number of excellent books on that topic already published. This book was written as a way to share the insights of the best in their field and the underlying psychological factors common to those elite achievers to create an urgent and competitive mindset. The field of sports and performance psychology is a dynamic industry, and the greatest days of knowledge and experience are yet to come. What that means for athletes, coaches, and those in the industry is that we are continually challenged to delve into the observations and standards to understand, learn, and deconstruct the pathways to success. This book is about learning to find your individual pathway as a high achiever and understanding the pathways of those you influence as a coach or parent.

As experiences go, elite human performance is truly unique. The pursuit of a goal changes the competitor in a way that can be both intoxicating and debilitating – even within the same day. What it takes is the ability of a competitor to lay it on the line, without hesitation, for a chance to succeed. Never guaranteed, always challenged.

Throughout life, a person's engagement with the environment never overshadows that individual's personal relationship with the things that make them tick and the things that create difficulty for them. Fighting for a challenge – whether that's making the team, winning the tournament, or overcoming a career-threatening injury – is purely unique to that person. The fears, doubts, and desires can never be managed by another – only by you.

Writing this book was a challenge for me. I was an athlete, but certainly not one who would have been called an "all-star." I was riddled with fear as a high school and collegiate athlete, and I look back now and wish I had better understood that emotion – why it was there and why I struggled to manage it. When I was scheduled to start as a pitcher, I would actually warm up at home by throwing into a homemade strike-zone apparatus, in a desperate effort to predict the kind of "command" I was going to have that evening. I was always searching, and that's probably why it took me so long to write this book; I was searching for a message, when I actually had the message all along. I just didn't believe it.

As an athlete, I always succeeded when my back was against the wall, and it was even better when no one expected anything of me. I loved being the underdog, because I had nothing to lose. As a pitcher – from Little League all the way through college – I struggled as a starter but flourished as a reliever. I only started one game in college (completely by choice), but otherwise, if coach asked me if I wanted to start a game, I would invariably beg him to let me stay in the bullpen. I was great if someone else had struggled and I was asked to come in and fix the problem, but the thought that I might have to set the tone for the game from the outset was scary as hell. My fears simply overran my desires.

The game is certainly hard, but life can be even harder. It is a brutal examination of every aspect of who we are and the interaction we have with the world around us. It is challenging yet glorious.

Success and failure are categorical definitions, not experiences. Experiences are reserved for the process and the journey. When we use categorical definitions, we suck the living out of life.

I chose to write this book after years of waiting and holding on to my thoughts because I was reluctant to open myself up to the vulnerabilities of being a writer. I have worked with the best, from champions to survivors, from warriors to lovers. In the end, they're all the same. The challenge may be different, but the calling is the same. That's where I sit with this book. There's a lot of apprehension attached to putting your heart and soul into a manuscript only to potentially miss the mark. My individual experience is about pleasing others and meeting their expectations, even though as a clinician and sports psychologist, I've always tried my best to keep my individual experiences out of the equation. Writing a book that delves into the philosophies that guide me is my challenge in life; it simply puts me out in front of those who I want to impact the most.

Elite human performance can be understood in many different ways. The measuring tools we use can be the same, but the application of these tools is what separates the various playing fields. And there is a purpose to these tools. A clicking clock, for example, serves to remind us of the order and experience of life. Regardless of what's going on in the outside world, the clock ticks to a rhythm that has been engineered to match the actual passing of time. Through each tick and each tock, life marches on.

Expert watch designers sit in small rooms in their workshops and design, refine, and improve the precision of their watches. An inexpensive watch can do the same thing as an expensive, handcrafted precision watch, but the value of the cheaper model is often tested when it matters the most. The inexpensive watch may not be engineered to handle tasks other than the strict measurement of time, but it still serves the purpose for which it was created. But when real precision and reliability in the face of uncertain environments is required, the craftsmanship and trustworthiness of a less expensive watch may be compromised, and this highlights the benefits of the precision and craftsmanship that are built into more expensive models. Nevertheless, each watch is created with a design of purpose and utility. Each watch has a purpose.

Humans are no different. Our hearts beat for a reason. But despite the fact that we're all equipped with a beating heart, we all have different rhythms. We're not the same, and our hearts don't beat in exactly the same way. Our individual purposes in life are much the same – I may not know what your purpose is or what someone else's may be, but the truth is that we all have one, and we don't get to find ours until we've fought through pain to test that "heartbeat" under pressure.

I do what I do because people fascinate me, and even more importantly, because I'm mesmerized by the human pursuit of goals and desires. It is never easy, and honestly, there are usually many more challenges than there are victories. The human experience is about struggles and learning, about managing the pain of the battle, the fear of the impending challenge, and the brief exhilaration of success. The struggle defines us. This book is now a part of me, and I hope it becomes a part of you.

Table of Contents

The
Calling

"In every successful athlete's career, there is a moment that happens in a game or practice that is painful, embarrassing, and possibly devastating to their long term success. What defines an athlete's future is not the details of that moment, but how they handle the psychological impact of that moment. Do they avoid the lesson and allow that moment to define them, or do they lean into it, face their fears, and fight through the adversity? That is the choice that is between growth and greatness or fear and failure."

– Dr. Bhrett McCabe

1

My Journey

I sat in the dugout angry and frustrated, lost in my thoughts and overwhelmed with doubts about who I was as a player. I had met my baseball idol one minute and let down my coach the next. Unfortunately, my poor performance was the norm rather than the exception. It was simply who I was, and in that moment, I had no idea how to change it.

As a member of the Louisiana State University baseball team, I wasn't your average player. I hadn't been heavily recruited. In fact, I hadn't made a single recruiting trip to any school before enrolling at LSU. I had played only one year of varsity baseball in high school, primarily because I was young, not very good, and in desperate need of the kind of seasoning that the junior varsity team could provide. When I met my teammates at LSU and read their accolades, I was embarrassed by the lack of anything in my bio other than "2nd Team All-District Senior Year in High School." I couldn't make first team all-district in high school, and yet here I was sitting in a locker room full of the top collegiate baseball players in the country. I was overwhelmed, but I was still hungry.

I was an invited walk-on, which meant that I was guaranteed a spot on the team but would be attending school on an academic rather than athletic scholarship. I had grown up as a baseball player, and all I wanted was a chance to compete in college, but I still wasn't completely sure if I had the guts to do it.

When the call came during my senior year of high school that LSU Coach Skip Bertman was interested in meeting me, I was excited but shocked. Coach Bertman had started a college baseball empire in Baton Rouge. My dad took the day off from work, and I checked out of school to drive across town and meet with Coach. As we sat in his office, he was direct and encouraging.

"You aren't good enough to play for me, not this year," he told me. "But I think you will be in two years, and I want to take a chance on you. You'll have to work hard, trust our process, trust the system, and be patient. If you do that, you'll succeed, more than the other pitchers you've competed against in high-school. But you have to buy in fully." Since I had no other offers to play at a college that matched my academic desires, the decision was easy.

As he laid out the plan for me to redshirt my freshman season but still be a vital part of the team by throwing batting practice and working out, my dad leaned over the desk and said one thing that I'll never forget: "Coach, I've worked 18 years to build him up to be in a position to take the responsibility. He's ready. All I ask is that you do what it takes to make Bhrett a man."

Coach leaned back in his chair and smiled. "Well, that's up to Bhrett," he said, "but I'll give him everything I have." I had no idea what that might entail, but I would find out four years later, on a night that changed my life.

But first a little background.

The morning after throwing in the last fall intrasquad game of the 1992 season, my third year in college, I woke with a sharp, stabbing pain in the front of my shoulder, which worsened when I tried to comb my hair. I thought it was just normal post-pitching pain, but a week later, when the discomfort hadn't lessened at all, I made an appointment with the orthopedic surgeon, who diagnosed it as shoulder tendinitis and instructed me to rest and rehabilitate. The timing couldn't have been worse: For the first time in my collegiate career, I was succeeding on the mound, even dominating.

The pain in my shoulder wasn't just physical – I was experiencing a lot of emotional distress as I pondered whether I'd be able to re-create the success I'd enjoyed that fall, and whether I'd be able to take on an even greater role in the upcoming season. Unfortunately, it didn't stop. I did exactly as the doctor ordered, but when I returned for spring camp, the pain and discomfort were still there. I secretly tried to alter my throwing motion to protect the shoulder, but that didn't help much. After just a few days of increased throwing, the staff shut me down for more rest. As the season approached, I desperately tried harder and harder to get back, but this, not surprisingly, only made things worse, and I would eventually only pitch about eleven innings that year. Although my personal performance was disappointing, the team managed to win its second national championship in three years. That accomplishment was certainly bittersweet for me – I had expected before the injury to play a much larger role on the pitching staff, but I suddenly found myself playing the same disappointing bit part that I'd toiled with in my first two seasons.

I had let an injury sideline me. But even though the physical injury appeared to be the culprit, the truth was that my *mental game* was terrible. That season, every one of my appearances was in relief during the middle of the week, normally against teams that were less competitive than the schools we faced in conference play. As the leader of a two-time national championship team that had won four consecutive conference championships in the toughest conference in the country, Coach always had a developmental plan, and although I was right in the middle of it, I felt stuck and unable to make any real positive progress. I would normally come in to relieve one of our struggling starting pitchers – I was very effective at getting out of jams that I hadn't created. But when the inning was over, I'd invariably sit in the dugout and worry about the next inning, and more specifically, about the first hitter of the next inning.

Let me explain.

At LSU, athletes enjoy an elite level of preparation, and we prided ourselves on doing things that other players, coaches, and programs simply did not or would not commit to doing. One of those things was something we called "Yellow Book" meetings. These get-togethers, which were normally held on Friday evenings from 7 to 9 in the offseason, were designed to study the statistical and psychological aspects of the game. It was a little overwhelming to sit in a meeting in October, four months before the season, and statistically break down the percentages of pitches thrown and how hitters respond to them. One of the most important statistics was the importance of the first hitter in an inning, and more importantly, what happened when a pitcher walked that leadoff hitter: Eighty percent of the time, the runner scored. I knew this statistic as well as anyone, and it made me panic.

When I returned to the mound after an often successful half-inning of relief work, I would test each warm-up pitch to make sure I could throw it for a strike, much as I used to do in my backyard before my high school games. I didn't do this because I was particularly interested in throwing strikes; I did it because I was definitely interested in not throwing balls and walking hitters. Unfortunately, any success I might have had with this strategy during warm-ups usually didn't carry over to game conditions, and walking hitters became a given for me. I would watch my velocity drop and the break on my breaking balls disappear. Not only was I a sitting duck, I was a sitting duck with an uncomfortable new throwing motion that had developed simply as a work-around to ease my shoulder pain. I had zero command or confidence. I sucked, and I knew it.

As my redshirt junior season (my fourth year in college) approached, my parents came up with a last-ditch option. They had learned of a man in town who practiced hypnotherapy and who had apparently helped a friend of theirs learn to meditate as a way to find peace in his life. I thought, "What do I have to lose?"

MacTavish "Mac" Williamson was a huge man of Northern Irish descent who had a strong accent that sang sentences in rhythm. He wasn't a therapist or a psychologist; he was a hypnotherapist, and he became my catalyst to succeed. His office was peaceful and comforting. He knew nothing about baseball, and no one knew that I went to see him several times a week. I would skip class and go get my mind right, then listen to tapes at night. Mac was my saving grace.

As the season approached, I found something in the bullpen during one late evening session. The bullpen isn't just a place where pitchers warm up during a game; it's a training ground, and the time you spend there can be one of refinement, frustration, or a combination of both. For me, Coach wasn't even present for most of my bullpen sessions even though he was our pitching coach – as the start of the season neared, he needed to work with the pitchers who were going to contribute, not with someone who was simply filling out a roster spot. I started to get used to my messed up throwing motion, and I eventually learned to throw a hard slider, a pitch that when thrown effectively looks just like a straight fastball but breaks away from the hitter at the last minute. Thanks to my strange new motion, the pitch was well hidden and worked brilliantly. Coach took notice and penciled me in to throw on the first weekend of the season.

In the second game of the year, in the New Orleans Superdome, I pitched the ninth inning and dominated. Two strikeouts and a ground out. Easy. But it was also the start of a new challenge for me. For the first time in 18 months, I was respected and valued again as a pitcher.

The next few games were hit and miss – decent but nothing special. That changed in March 1994, when I found myself sitting in the dugout one night after meeting my idol, about to face the fears that had driven me throughout my athletic career. I had never been challenged by a coach like this before, and though there was a purpose behind it, I didn't know it at the time.

That idol was Nolan Ryan. The hard-throwing right-hander was country strong and rancher mean. He was the game's all-time strikeout leader, and he had thrown a staggering seven no-hitters over his 27-year pro career, even defying the odds and Father Time by throwing his last no-no at the age of 44. He was also something of a jerk on the mound, and I loved that.

Ryan was in Baton Rouge to watch his son pitch against us for Texas Christian University (TCU). Before the game, all of our pitchers had gathered around the dugout for a chance to meet Ryan and shake his hand. We were raving fans, and we acted like it, but when he finally made it to our dugout, he was very businesslike and to the point. He did sign a ball for me, however, and I still have it in my office today.

In the fifth inning, I was brought in to bail us out of a jam. The bases were loaded with Horned Frogs, and there were no outs. Ryan was sitting about a hundred feet away, watching my every move as I walked to the mound. This was a potentially ugly situation, but relief was always fun for me, and I managed to retire the side without allowing a run. I ran off the field with excitement and pride as a completely sold-out Alex Box Stadium erupted and cheered me on. To my surprise, Coach Bertman was waiting for me at the white lines.

As I approached, he put his arms on my shoulders and started talking. Coach believed that when you had something important to tell a player, you did one of two things – you either put your hands on his shoulders, so he knew you were trying to make a connection with him, or you kept talking until he blinked three times. Both methods let him know that you were listening and absorbing his message.

That night, his message was direct. "Do you want the good news or the bad news?" he asked. I actually thought the bad news would be that he was taking me out of the game, which, to be honest, would have been great – I would have been able to do a good job and then get yanked before I had to do it again. Unfortunately, he didn't let me off that easy. The good news, he said, was that my performance that inning was the best he had ever seen from me. The bad news? If I walked the leadoff hitter in the next inning, he was taking me out of the game.

I remember looking at him as though he were both crazy and cruel. No coach would ever implant a negative outcome in a player's mind. Isn't that exactly what every sports psychology book advocates *against?*

As our hitters were batting in the bottom half of the inning, I was sitting in the dugout thinking two things: how wrong Coach was, and how I would show him that I wasn't going to walk the leadoff guy. Between innings, we pitchers were normally allowed to throw six warm-up pitches. When I took the mound in the top of the next inning, I tested each of those pitches as I loosened up to see if I could throw them for strikes. Encouragingly, I was six for six. But for some reason, I was also more nervous than I'd ever been.

The leadoff hitter stepped into the box, and the battle began. No one else knew about the conversation I'd had with Coach, but if anyone had known, I would have confirmed their suspicions pretty quickly that I was scared to death. The first pitch was high but right over the middle of the plate. The second pitch was in the exact same location. The third pitch should have been called a strike, but the umpire missed the call. And the fourth pitch was ball four. Not only had I walked the leadoff hitter, I'd walked him on four pitches. As I took the throw back from the catcher, I walked behind the mound to re-gather myself. That's when I noticed that Coach was coming out to the mound. He had already made the signal to the bullpen. I was done.

When he got to me, on the mound in front of a capacity crowd, he told me I simply didn't have the chops to pitch at LSU. I was done for the weekend. As soon as I handed the ball to the pitcher replacing me, I ran into the dugout and punched a metal bench, put a towel over my head, and pouted. After an inning or two of sulking, I decided that since I now officially sucked as a pitcher, I could at least cheer on my teammates.

After the game, my dad walked up to me to find out why I had been taken out of the game so quickly. I told him what had happened. Instead of getting angry with Coach, he told me that he agreed with him, and that I just had to be better. The worst part came after the game: Nolan Ryan credited the rest of our staff for the victory; he didn't say a word about how I had managed to get the team out of such a hard jam.

The next morning, I was sent with six other pitchers who weren't scheduled to pitch that day to do a clinic about an hour away from campus. This was pretty common early in the year, and it was a great way to build community enthusiasm and engagement. We were listening to the game on the ride back when our graduate assistant decided to stop at McDonald's for lunch. College athletes are never afraid of free food, and since I wasn't going to pitch anymore that weekend, I took him up on the offer. We picked up the food and continued back to campus, and as we pulled into the stadium parking lot, still scarfing down our burgers, it became clear that our starting pitcher – an All-American who had dominated in the national championship game the year before – was struggling. As I walked into the stadium, our equipment manager grabbed me and told me to get to the bullpen to get loose. I had to run into the locker room and get my spikes on, even though I had none of my other necessities (e.g., cup, ankle tape, undershirt) and no time to change. I did find enough time for one more bite of my sandwich, however. Nutrition matters.

As soon as I got loose, I entered the game. I had inherited runners on second and third and no outs. But true to form, I struck out the side. Needless to say, I was more than a little excited as I ran off the field, but this time, it was more about proving to Coach that I was effective, that my last outing hadn't broken me. To my shock, he once again met me at the white lines and delivered the exact same comments.

I just looked at him with disgust.

As I sat in the dugout, I made sure that a few teammates knew what was going on. My roommate, a three-year All-American, College

Baseball Hall of Famer, and longtime major leaguer, walked over and told me to forget it. I looked at him and told him in the most defeated way possible that I was trying. As I headed back out to the mound for the next inning, I once again tested my warm-up pitches. And sure enough, I was again six for six.

When the hitter stepped into the box, I walked him on five pitches, and this time, not one of them really sniffed the strike zone. The only called strike I got was a gift from the umpire. As I walked behind the mound to find my happy spot, I was surprised to see that Coach hadn't come out of the dugout. He was going to let me work through it, something that all pitchers feel they should be given the chance to do. The next hitter stepped into the box and promptly drove the first pitch off the wall for a run-scoring double. As soon as the ball hit the bat, Coach was on his way out of the dugout and my chance was over. I swear he nearly collided with the batter charging down the first-base line. He told me that I was too scared to pitch at LSU, that he needed guys who were committed, not afraid. He was right.

The following Monday, I went back to Mac and had a sit-down with him. I told him what had happened and explored what I thought was the answer. Mac listened intently, but then simply asked me a question that may have changed my life: "What did you want to achieve when you were pitching?"

It was a loaded question, and all I could think of to say was, "Not what I've been doing." At that moment, I realized that I had been just trying to survive, not succeed.

He told me that the mind only functions at an elite level when it's locked into its desires, not when it's working to avoid its fears. If I had the chance to pitch without fear, he asked, what would I like to do on the mound? I told him that without question, I'd like to strike out every hitter I faced, but that I was afraid to commit to that because I might overthrow and end up walking hitters. It was more comfortable to play it safe. He leaned back, and asked me again in his Irish brogue if my current strategy was working, or whether it might be worth the risk to trust myself and stop playing it safe?

Once again, it was a great question, and I made up my mind that day to try to strike out every hitter I faced going forward. What did I have to lose?

The next few appearances were eye-opening. I pitched really well, and I had a different mentality on the mound. The competition was a notch below what we would face from our conference opponents, but nevertheless, I was succeeding. Strikeouts and scoreless innings had become the norm. And as conference play began, my role continued to increase. I was always the first pitcher out of the pen, regardless of inning. I relished the role and was confident.

Throughout that season, as I perfected my crazy throwing motion, I had one goal: strikeouts. I loved them – so much so that if the hitter hit a soft ground ball for an out, I was upset. I knew I could dominate the opposing hitters with strikeouts, and it made it even worse for them when they saw that, by and large, I was much less of a physical player than they were. But as far as I was concerned, I was committed, and they weren't.

In the conference tournament later that season, I entered in relief and saved the first game. In the second game, I entered the game in the eighth, with the bases loaded, no outs, and us up by a run. As I had done in March, I managed to wriggle out of the situation without a run crossing the plate. I even gave up a hit to start the ninth and was replaced, but this time it didn't matter – I knew I had done my job. In the post-game news conference, Coach singled me out, recalling my difficulties in the March game and what I had learned to do since then. It was as though the whole thing was playing out according to a script. And that's because it was.

I finished the season pitching in the College World Series, an absolute dream come true. My statistics were at the top of the conference in a variety of categories, and I was honored with the Most Improved Player award at our annual team banquet. The only glitch came when our academic advisor told me at the banquet that I earned a "D" in the class that I kept skipping to go see Mac. Give and take, I guess.

After that season, I changed my major to psychology. I wanted to know why I had felt the way I had in the dugout when I was pitching so poorly, and how I could change that for myself and others. When I finished my final season, I pursued a graduate degree in clinical psychology. Sports psychology simply wasn't enough; I was more interested in studying the complexities of human behavior and the human experience, and athletics lacked the kind of depth I was looking for. It was a great decision.

Over the next eight years, I completed my training in clinical psychology, specializing in the interplay of medical conditions and the psychological experience. Thanks to my time struggling with my own injuries and learning to overcome them, my curiosity and interest in this field was piqued.

Several years ago, I finally sat down with Coach at his house. Former players usually look forward to these often intense but intimate conversations with their one-time mentors. I told him that he was one of three people – my mom and my dad were the other two – who had changed my life and shaped my pathway to success. He told me that he was only doing what my dad had asked him to do at that first meeting. He remembered the meeting to the smallest details – what my father was wearing, and obviously, what he had said. I asked him if he knew the day my life had changed, and he quickly recalled the specific conversation we had had on the mound in March 1994. He remembered it to the day, the game, and the inning.

My mindset shifted that day from passive and hopeful to aggressive, intentful, and determined. That day, *The MindSide Manifesto* was born.

2

The Manifesto

The importance of why my life changed that night in 1994 has become clear and serves as the impetus for this book. Prior to that night, I was good at things, but never very successful at achieving the things that I really wanted. I was an average student who always seemed to find the easy way out but still had a B-grade average. To me, success was just getting by, and I was never really committed to fighting for my desires. But I discovered that "good enough" was no longer good enough – it simply wasn't fulfilling anymore to just get by.

The drastic change in my mental perspective may have been spiritual or divine, but I'll never know that for certain. What I do know, however, is that by simply changing my mindset, I changed my life.

My story doesn't involve overcoming addiction or prevailing through horrendous life circumstances. When I hear speakers or read books about those who have persevered through supremely difficult life challenges, I often feel inadequate – surely the difficulties presented to me by my less than ideal mindset could never measure up to the real tragedies and hardships encountered by those people. Nevertheless, that evening changed me – deeply.

When I sat in Mac's office, the message he delivered to me was deeper than the game of baseball, but as is the case with so many athletes I work with, the game was a vehicle to greater personal understanding. At the time, I really thought I was living a fully engaged life and was committed to my desires. I was playing baseball for the best collegiate baseball program in the country, in my hometown, in front of my parents, and in front of my friends, many of whom doubted that I would succeed at LSU. But I know now that I was simply getting by, and that had to change.

Looking back on those days, I realize that I needed a significant mindset shift if I was going to give up the safety nets and security blankets that I had made my standards. I had to be exposed and vulnerable to success and failure. The obsessive fear about whether I had what it took to perform had to be overcome, but the only way that was going to happen was if I attempted, failed, and learned. My fear of success was so much more powerful than my fear of failure. My heart and rear-end needed to be put on the line and forced to risk everything if I truly wanted to succeed.

The biggest change would have to take place inside. I had to declare to myself what I wanted, how I was going to achieve it, and what I was willing to do to get there. Simply dreaming about it was no longer enough – good breaks were not going to just come my way, the heavens were not going to open and make it happen for me, and no particular game – no matter how well I played – was going to suddenly spark my confidence. I had to determine what I truly wanted and exactly how I was going to get there.

A manifesto is a public declaration of ideas, positions, and intent. For many, the word has a negative connotation, because it's often used to describe a declaration of ideas issued by a dangerous dictator or a political group. I'm challenging you here to think beyond that meaning. For me, a manifesto is merely a platform or philosophy that you believe in so strongly that you're willing to declare it publicly.

My manifesto became my daily support system. It was no longer permissible to be good enough, to accept the status quo, or to simply be a part of the team or life. I finally began to believe in my purpose every day, even though I had no idea at first how much this would impact my life and career.

As I entered my redshirt junior season in 1994, I was a business major, plugging along with a 2.8 grade point average and a vague desire to attend law school. With a semester left to graduation, I wasn't particularly worried about my grades – I just figured I'd do extremely well in the standardized assessment testing required for law school admission. The problem was that even though I had the study materials and planned to take the test, I never actually started studying, never bothered with the law school application process, and never researched the schools that I might be interested in. The desire was to go to law school, but the effort, as usual, was just doing enough to get by.

After the 1994 season, I changed my major, a particularly risky move for a student who had one semester left before graduation. I decided to completely shift gears and switch to psychology, even though the only psychology class I had taken to that point had been a complete disaster. As a sophomore, I had enrolled in a night class called Introduction to Psychology. I despised the course – the subject matter wasn't very interesting to me, and I skipped class more often than I showed up. At the mid-term, I was failing. But then I got lucky – I came down with a fairly serious case of mononucleosis and missed the final six weeks of the semester. This conveniently allowed me to complete the course via an independent study that summer. And even *then* I struggled to pass. Just getting by, right?

This time, my foray into psychology would be different, because I had experienced, first-hand, the power of human psychology, elite performance, and the development of my personal manifesto. I was thirsty for the information. I met with my academic advisor and she quickly changed my major, but she made it clear that getting into graduate school at LSU was a long shot, because grad schools often frown upon the practice of accepting applicants from their own undergraduate programs, simply to avoid watering down the diversity of the student body. Okay, challenge accepted.

I never made less than a 3.75 GPA after changing my major, and while it required an additional two semesters to finish my undergraduate degree, I finished the last two semesters in unprecedented fashion for me with a 4.0. I thoroughly studied for the graduate admission tests and worked with anyone I could in the psychology department to learn and to gain connections. Thankfully, I met a professor who was looking for a graduate student, and contingent upon my performance on the standardized tests, I was able to interview for admission. Things fell into place for me, and I started graduate school the following fall at LSU.

My graduate school experience came with different challenges and blessings, but I was fully engaged and invested in succeeding. All I wanted was a chance to learn, grow, and compete. From LSU to a clinical psychology internship conducted in association with the Brown University Medical School, my hunger and desire were always greater than my "ability," but I was determined not to stop until I learned what I wanted to learn and met the people that I wanted to meet. Fortunately, amazing professors at LSU such as Drs. William Waters and Philip Brantley, and at Brown with Drs. Alan Sirota and Justin Nash, challenged me but never tried to discourage my goals. My goals were different, but they understood my desires and drive and encouraged me throughout training.

My manifesto changed me. It forced me to declare, without apology or safety nets, that I was all-in on my goals. I wasn't afraid to share my dreams and desires, but I also didn't need approval from anyone in my life. My wife and my parents were well aware of my dreams, and they thankfully supported them without question. From that day back in 1994, I found a much deeper purpose to my life. Without Coach challenging me, Mac providing guidance, and my family supporting me, I would have walked through life without much of a purpose. My purpose wasn't about changing the world; it was about changing me to be a better, more successful person for the world.

This book, *The MindSide Manifesto*, was written to highlight the things I've learned over the course of my journey. Remember, I don't have an amazing, breathtaking story of redemption or perseverance. Mine is one of finding the purpose within and then declaring it to the man standing in the mirror. In the following chapters, I'm going to review numerous aspects of human psychology, including the factors that help guide those who are succeeding and the challenges that face those who are struggling to find their purpose. Every day, I have to come to grips with the same concepts reviewed in this book and to work to address them without certainty. I challenge you to explore the psychological aspects covered here and to examine and question your underlying beliefs.

"Good enough" is simply not acceptable anymore. Your life isn't about surviving life's difficulties; it's about taking full advantage of the opportunities you get to learn, grow, and succeed. Failures will happen, but only through failure is learning possible. One can't be present without the potential for the other. Only when you accept that will you succeed.

Be patient as you wait for the growth that will come from your own manifesto. If what you desire is important enough to fight for, it won't come easily or quickly. Be engaged in the journey, and start the process as soon as you can. Your mental approach to life deserves a manifesto. Doesn't it?

3

The Mental Game

When you connect to the mental side, you connect to the person. We are all dynamic, living, breathing creatures. Beneath the desire to succeed lie the doubts, hopes, and desires of a person simply trying to do something good. It doesn't matter what that something is, as long as it is something.

The current psychological framework in sports is at a crossroads – it's somewhere between pop science and traditional science and how the two interact. As a psychologist, I'm trained to see the complexities of the human experience, to see how things trigger and influence factors in our lives, and to see how those same things are reinforced, extinguished, and maintained, and how they influence our thoughts, feelings, and actions. Unfortunately, psychologists and other human behavioral experts are typically poor at communicating and disseminating material to the masses. The theories are convoluted and sometimes abstract. So what happens is the emergence of thought leaders who often take one aspect, make it seem relevant, and leverage the one philosophy that helped them personally as they try to answer to all – often as they live with a confirmation bias of their own.

The mental game is much more than platitudes, motivational quotes, and positive affirmations. Understanding human behavior is the start of it all, and appreciating how the person, more than just the athlete, interacts with environmental challenges is critical.

When the personal experience of a mental coach is shifted to a platform that's designed to serve everyone, the mental coach is making a huge error by not understanding the player, the coach, and the game, from individuals up to the entire organization. It's a common error, and no different than what is commonly seen in the weight-loss marketplace. A person starts out on his or her own journey to find a healthier, better way of eating. Over time, this journey results in a significant change in health. As a result, what worked for that individual suddenly becomes the "right way" for everyone, and as a result, he or she becomes the sign-carrying, flag-waving platform spokesperson. "If you have diabetes, this way of eating is perfect for you. Thyroid issues? This works for that, too. Hypertension? No problem." And so on.

We are not all the same. Every one of us comes from a different background, a different upbringing, and equipped with a different vision of the world. To suggest that something is universal – whether that something is a diet or a mental approach – is ignorant and dangerous. It may have merit, it may have relevance, and it may be beneficial, but it is NEVER universal.

The mental game in sports is no exception. The goal is to find YOUR path by incorporating the knowledge and experiences of others into your OWN journey. It's important to question everything and explore alternative forms of thought. Without exploration, the mind becomes stagnant, and a stagnant mind is a dying mind.

I've been fortunate to work with some of the world's best in their particular sport. I watch great athletes struggle with the same difficulties encountered by my junior athletes, and I watch them get as excited for victories as the child who wins his or her first game. While our pathways and psychological frameworks are different, many traits are common to elite performers and high achievers. How an individual learns from them is the key lesson.

For me, being a licensed clinical psychologist who specializes in sports and performance is an awesome responsibility. Human behavior is not only important, it's critical to success. The brain is such an amazing organ, and we learn more and more about its true potential every day.

A coach asked me recently why we've begun to see so many psychologists and mental coaches entering the sports and performance industry. It's a great question, so I asked Lanny Basham, a prominent mental coach and Olympic gold medal–winner, what he thought. Basham suggested that the involvement is way overdue. He told me that when he talks to large groups of coaches, they almost unanimously cite the importance of the mind to human performance. When he asks how many have formal programs for training the mental side of the game, however, the room often goes silent.

The reason we're seeing such an explosion in the industry is that the coaching and athletic marketplace is demanding more and more access to insights and strategies devoted to maximizing human performance. The industry is changing – it's moving away from the corrective nature of fixing troubled and struggling athletes to a more constructive role, working with athletes before anything major goes wrong. With milliseconds separating championships, it's beneficial to find any and every opportunity to gain an advantage on your competition. Strength and conditioning experts are trusted from the earliest stages of an athlete's development to help the player reach elite status, so why wouldn't the same apply to mental coaches?

Human psychology is centered on understanding how an individual's thoughts, emotions, and interaction with the environment impact his or her psychological well-being. Sports psychology is the application of human psychological principles to the sporting environment. The thoughts, feelings, fears, motivations, and efforts that we direct toward preparation, competition, and post-recovery are all influenced by the others. It's a beautifully complex matrix that can still be influenced by the choices of the athlete.

The MindSide, the name of my company and the name of my overall perspective on human performance, is about understanding the interplay of these factors for the athlete. It was formed by combining my personal experiences as an athlete and a person with my experience as a psychologist. What I found most fascinating were the uncertainties involved in the study of human behavior. There are no definites and no absolutes. Every athlete who walks through the door has a unique background that influences his or her perception, goals, and mindset. To assume otherwise completely misses the individuality that makes this world special.

It is often said that sports are a microcosm of life. In the heat of the moment, the game doesn't care who you are, where you're from, the color of your skin, or what you believe in. It only demands effort, teamwork, and commitment to challenge in order to succeed.

Throughout this book, you'll learn the various aspects of The MindSide and how it may impact your performance and your manifesto. This isn't the only way, but it is a way that will hopefully shine a light and guide you as you incorporate the principles and understanding needed to become a true champion, on and off the field. For me, the perspective-my drive to compete and grow through life- became as powerful as my manifesto, my drive to compete and grow through life. It consumed me, and my hope is that you, too, will see that growth and interest within you.

The Psychological Barriers to Success –
Understanding What Builds Your Manifesto

"It is not about developing the perfect game plan for success. Rather, it is about having the psychological maturity to develop plans for when adversity, mediocrity, and frustration hit. Having a trusted plan and the ability to shift focus away from fixing the problems that are occurring and onto the steps to persevere through all challenges is what defines champions."

– Dr. Bhrett McCabe

4

Finding the Aspects to Build Your Manifesto

Knowing where to start when building a house is difficult, particularly if you've never built one before. You have to find the land, survey the property, lay the foundation, and secure the support throughout the house. Without the early work, the finishing steps would be built on a poor foundation, risking long-term collapse.

There is a great team-building exercise that I conduct when I'm with new teams. It reinforces the importance of having a vision and a plan, because without both, the vision simply becomes a guess.

When the teams arrive in the conference room, I've already laid out two or three piles of Legos on different tables. None of the piles have pictures or instructions to identify what the pieces should be used to build or any suggestions about the overall formula. I simply tell each team to start building and see what they can create. It's always interesting to see the creativity demonstrated by the teams, but they always seem to create something that's fairly close to the general theme of the original box – either a small dump truck or a police car depending on their table

After some good fun, I ask the groups if there's anything that I could have given them that would have made their job easier. Almost invariably, they simply want to know what they're supposed to be building. Rarely do they ask for instructions. So then I give them the boxes from which the individual Lego piles were taken and ask them to start building again.

This is where things often get interesting. As it turns out, having a picture to guide them as they build often causes more difficulty than having no guidance at all. The groups often try to fit the pieces they have in front of them to the picture, but then become frustrated and angry when the two don't match. So what's the point? Having a vision is a necessary step, but without a plan, the individual parts become confusing.

To finish the exercise, I provide them with instructions, with which they're quickly able to complete the exercise. That's when I'll often overhear comments such as, "Oh, so *that's* what that piece is for!" or "I had no idea what to do with this, but now it makes sense." It's a powerful exercise that helps reinforce the importance of having a vision, a plan, and a commitment to execute the plan.

When my life changed, it was sparked by my commitment to my manifesto. I was completely unaware of the challenges that I had faced before that, and I wasn't really aware of the aspects of my life, both in sport and outside the game, that were causing me difficulty. But with the manifesto in place, I had the energy needed to create a plan that would help me achieve the vision.

Building your manifesto requires understanding exactly which pieces you would leave on the table if you didn't have an instruction manual. More importantly, it requires an understanding of the most important pieces in your life. And don't forget – it's often the little pieces that don't seem to fit into your life or don't seem particularly consequential that can cause tremendous, life-altering foot pain when they litter your path to the bathroom at two o'clock in the morning. (If you have kids, you know what I'm talking about.) I think we could end wars simply by making armies walk barefoot in the dark across randomly scattered Legos.

It's important to understand how the psychological concepts that you see as strengths in others may simply be areas that need improvement in your life. Over the next few chapters, I'll review some of the important topics that I found to be helpful for my manifesto, many of which I simply had to grow through or find out about the hard way. More importantly, many of the themes addressed in this book are the common requests when clients seek out my services, so it's important to review them proactively. They're all critical to the human experience.

By reviewing these aspects of human performance, I've found that understanding how they relate to your own experience can bring you knowledge, perspective, and wisdom, all of which can enrich your overall engagement with life, competition, and existence. These are by no means exhaustive, but gaining understanding and appreciation for them can only help deepen your experience.

5

The Performance Map – The Game Plan

I'm often asked to describe my personal performance philosophy. While that's something that people who are competing and training should possess, it's also important for people like me – sports psychologists and mental coaches – to have an underlying philosophy of what impacts and influences human performance. As a clinical psychologist, I try to look at the core essence of people and the way they interact with their environment. Their thoughts, their feelings, and their emotions intertwine and work in unison, but never randomly. The whole thing functions in a systematic, connected manner.

My game plan for human performance starts with the person and how that person interacts with their competitive environment; how they train; and most importantly, how they overcome challenges. As a clinical psychologist, my strategy is an adaptation of the behavioral formulation I use to assess patients; it's an attempt to understand the various influences that impact their psychological well-being.

Several years ago, I created an infographic designed to give my clients a better understanding of the performance framework, and this was when the Game Plan was created. I want you to understand that at the core of all competitive environments, training situations, and adversity settings is you. As the athlete, YOU are the single most important factor in creating the outcomes that YOU want. Nobody can do it for you, and nobody will make it easier for you.

What matters is you and the way that you interact with the world. In that interaction, thoughts, feelings, and emotions are impacted, and the challenge is to work through the various levels of thought and emotion to succeed. If you understand that you are the coordinator and the center of the entire spectrum around you, you can improve your overall competitive mindset in a more effective and efficient manner. Too often, we look outside to coaches, or teachers, or situations and environments to make things easier for us or hand us the solutions. A person who lacks the self-confidence to be great and the self-confidence to overcome challenges invariably looks for fixes and solutions from others, rather than searching for the answers within.

A coach can inspire you and have an impact on you, and a great game can help bring confidence, but none of that can happen unless you have an understanding that you are (1) capable of succeeding and (2) ready to take on the challenge. Creating success is about timing and the consistent engagement of your actions. When it comes to whether or not you're going to succeed, you are the ultimate deciding factor.

You must accept that success can be defined on many different levels. Not everyone can be a champion, but everyone can work to achieve a championship mindset, and everyone can work to fight through the challenges that are necessary to become a champion. That's how you grow.

The Game Plan and the Power of Self-Belief:

The Game Plan was developed to help athletes understand that the way they feel about themselves and the way they interact with the world are intertwined. It's a bottom-up, not a top-down approach. [See next page]

It's true that a lot of great athletes are actually insecure, but that can be a positive thing, because it can help drive future performance. If an athlete is overly confident or comfortable with their status, they'll often stop training and working because the underlying "need" to get better is absent. When we see confidence, we often mistake that for arrogance. Confidence is knowing who you are and what you're capable of. Arrogance is saying, "I don't need to do anything else, because I already have everything I've ever needed."

THE
game plan 📍

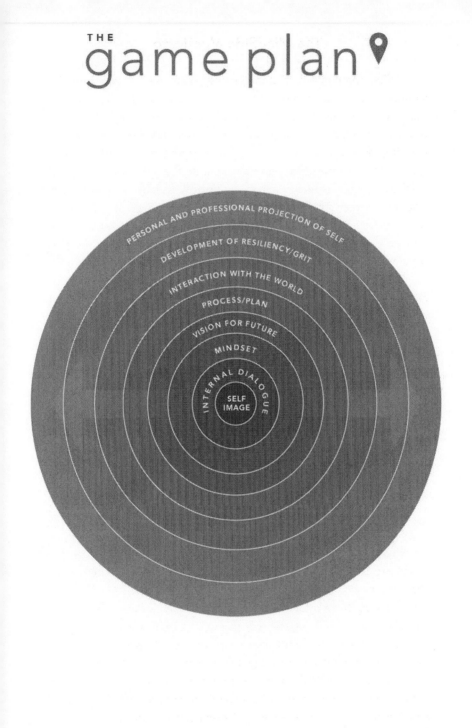

PERSONAL AND PROFESSIONAL PROJECTION OF SELF

DEVELOPMENT OF RESILIENCY/GRIT

INTERACTION WITH THE WORLD

PROCESS/PLAN

VISION FOR FUTURE

MINDSET

INTERNAL DIALOGUE

SELF IMAGE

There are multiple layers within the Game Plan. At the center is you and how you perceive yourself – your self-image. Self-image is the single-most important factor in the entire Game Plan model. I've never worked with athletes who have a low self-image and low self-confidence but still consistently drive results. Insecurity may be beneficial in the short term, but in the long run, it's hard to continually overcome insecurity and succeed. It ultimately comes down to one question: "Do you believe that you can achieve the challenges that are before you?"

Doubts are okay, because they can help drive future performance, but the athlete must inherently understand and appreciate that they are capable of achieving what they desire. Only when belief overtakes doubt does an athlete progress consistently and positively. Unfortunately, doubt grows like a weed, and belief requires structured farming. It's a constant battle. This will be discussed in detail in "The Mountain of Belief" chapter further on in the book.

In traditional, academic psychological literature, Dr. Albert Bandura famously coined the term "self-efficacy," which is the belief that you can overcome and succeed through a challenge.[1] Self-efficacy arises from self-image, which drives success. We build our self-image and the ability to achieve a task or a challenge in everything we do. It's the very core of you – your self-determined traits, capabilities, and representations. In practice and in training, you're building not only your skillsets, but your belief that you can overcome challenges in the future. If you believe you can, you will. Your self-image is influenced by your experiences, and the positive experiences of your past can help your self-image become constructive in nature.

Constructive experiences help you build an inventory and a library of positive engagement and success that moves from layer to layer and challenge to challenge. When we're faced with increasingly difficult challenges, great athletes draw upon their memories of past achievements and their reserves of positive self-image to subconsciously build enough self-efficacy to meet the current demands. And while negative experiences can be detrimental to our ego, they also help form resiliency. A person with a strong self-image understands that in both positive and negative environments, it's always possible to successfully meet demands that others may not be able to fulfill.

What do I mean by this? As I like to say, I want my pilots to fly better in bad weather than they can in good weather. When I board an airplane, I don't want a pilot who doubts his or her ability to successfully land the airplane in the rain, wind, snow, or in a thunderstorm. I want someone who has trained over and over again, who's been through a variety of environments, and who trusts that their self-image will allow them to handle the uncertain environment they're about to face. I don't want overconfidence and arrogance, but I do want a confident self-image and the belief that given the challenges ahead, the likelihood is good that they'll be able to meet the demands. The people around you can also help shape and form your self-image. It's much better, not surprisingly, to surround yourself with people who help build you up rather than tear you down.

However, it's also important to understand the distinction between people who tear you down and coaches who give critical feedback and constructive guidance, even if that feedback makes you feel less confident in the short term. You have to be clear about why a particular coaching criticism is coming your way and how you, as an athlete, can persevere to reach the desired outcome. Coaching is there to help influence, challenge, and get you to focus on the things that you need to do to get better. Part of the plan is to build up rather than break down who you are. If you don't take a step back and keep that in mind, you'll lose the opportunity to develop your self-image.

Do you measure up to your ideals? We all have role models and mentors in the sporting world with whom we identify, whether it's Tiger Woods, Michael Jordan, Brett Favre, Peyton Manning, or, in my case, Nolan Ryan. We all identify with individuals and try to take aspects of their personality and their image into our own. It's a fair question and a beneficial exercise. As long as you can see that you don't have to become those individuals, that you just have to learn from them, you'll contribute to the development of your self-image. A strong positive self-image doesn't simply just happen. It's not magic, and it doesn't happen overnight. It is built, developed, and grown through systematic training and awareness of what you're doing.

The hardest exercise for anyone is to look into the mirror and be honest with what you see in the reflection. So many people, not just athletes, have inaccurate images about who they are and how they interact with the world, and they're simply fooling themselves. To look in the mirror and be honest takes trust and a commitment to be honest with yourself. The truth is exactly who you are, with no filters, no hiding from the fact. From there, growth starts.

An Internal Dialogue:

Your self-image influences your internal dialogue. The voice that's constantly running through your head – the second layer of the Game Plan that builds out from your self-image – is the internal dialogue. We have two types of voices in life and in competition: a teammate voice and an opponent voice. Your teammate voice typically consists of supportive self-talk. That doesn't mean it's always positive, but it is always supportive. The communication of that teammate voice is designed to get you motivated and focused on the challenge at hand.

It's important to understand that sometimes, even in your own internal dialogue, you have to rally the troops and raise the intensity. To do that, we sometimes have to ask ourselves hard questions. A teammate helps build positive mental approaches by understanding what is capable and how to achieve it. It's not *if*, it's *how*. The question should never be "Can we face this challenge?" Instead, it should be, "How will we face this challenge, and what resources do we have to do that?" The teammate voice is about learning, growing, and development.

The flip side of the teammate voice is the destructive opponent voice, which consumes many athletes. Competitors often have what are referred to in psychology as automatic negative thoughts. These are thoughts that tend to group together in themes that range from the catastrophization of outcomes, to the magnification of mistakes, to attempts to predict the future, and so on. These automatic thoughts breed in a culture of negativity, fear, doubt, and insecurity. You don't necessarily choose them, but they do seem to run in packs. When fear and doubt rise up from a negative self-image, the opponent voice grows louder and louder.

The doubts in the back of your mind and the consistently negative thoughts that arise in that perspective make it very difficult to focus on positive approaches and outcomes. Instead, your thoughts become more categorically focused on how you can't be successful. It's just another example of branding your unsuccessful nature rather than understanding how to apply the tools at your disposal. The opponent voice not only results in automatic negative thoughts, it's also built on irrational belief systems. The most common irrational beliefs that I hear from athletes who are fueled by an opponent voice and a low self-image are things such as "If I work hard, I'll succeed," or "The best always win."

It's important to understand that the world isn't fair – the best athletes don't always win, and the athletes who do everything right also don't always win. Sometimes those who take shortcuts or don't work as hard as you do end up on top of the mountain in victory. It's not fair, but it is reality. The challenges you face as an athlete build your self-image, which allows you to fuel the teammate self-talk and internal dialogue rather than allowing the opponent to have open season on your emotions. The teammate voice is constructive and developmental; the opponent voice is destructive and negative.

You can be aware of your self-talk and your internal dialogue and shape it for the future. You may not be able to change thoughts but you can change the environment from which the thoughts originate. That always comes back to your perception of who and what you are as an athlete and a person. If you have a negative self-image, you're creating a fertile ground for opponent-style negative self-talk to flourish. Enhance your self-image to encourage and foster a positive self-talk environment. An internal dialogue influences your mindset.

Mindset:

Over the last several years, we've gained an increased understanding of mindset thanks to the work of Stanford researcher and psychologist, Dr. Carol Dweck. Dr. Dweck has written extensively on the academic mindset of students who face challenges and overcome obstacles, categorizing two types of mindsets that are important in that environment. The application of her work has since been successfully extended to sports, business and the performing arts, as detailed in her book *Mindset: The New Psychology of Success.*[2]

A mindset is the lens through which you see the world and the way in which that lens rallies your internal resources to meet challenges and demands. It affects how you deal with failure, how you prepare for success, and how you rise up to challenges. It always arises from self-belief and your self-image, and is a common indicator used to differentiate between consistent success and failure.

There are two types of mindsets that help determine how you approach the world around you: the *fixed mindset* and the *growth mindset*. They're polar opposites, and I think it's important to accept the fact that we, as athletes and people, may fall somewhere in the middle. There may be aspects of us on one side of the coin and different aspects on the other. It's not about being all or nothing; it's about understanding how we can improve the way we see the world. The first mindset what is called a *fixed mindset*.

As Dr. Dweck conceptualizes, a *fixed mindset* tends to be fueled by a negative self-image or a lack of confidence in one's self-image. An athlete with a *fixed mindset* sees the challenges and experiences around them as validations of who they are, as a proving ground for his or her inherent capabilities. This increases the pressure to be successful, simply because success now determines whether or not they are good people. People with *fixed mindsets* often avoid challenges; any effort is usually just a by-product of the individual's inherent capabilities and talent. People who operate in a *fixed mindset* world are more concerned with proving than they are with growing.

Nevertheless, *fixed mindset* athletes can be very successful. I've seen it at every level of athletic competition (without mentioning specific examples to not call out those athletes), because early in the process, a *fixed mindset* can be important and effective. If you inherently believe in who you are, and you possess a certain skillset that is fixed – as though you were simply born with the capability to be successful – you can overcome those who might be considered inherently less talented. There is confidence in feeling that you were born a certain way; it's almost a form of athletic royalty. The problem with a *fixed mindset* comes when the environment is not predictive and the uncertain nature of competition demands more than just talent. Driven by a low self-image, *fixed-mindset* athletes can become easily frustrated and quickly abandon strategies and techniques that have helped them in the past, simply because the strategy isn't working and isn't maximizing their talent.

The opposite end of the spectrum is the *growth mindset*, which reflects a more positive self-image and is a more constructive performance mindset. A *growth mindset* accepts that everything that we do is learning and growth-dependent. The opportunities and challenges in life and sport are only vehicles for improvement. It's not about proving an underlying ability or skillset, it's about using the challenges and opportunities to continue to develop into the best version of themselves they can be, in sports and in life.

Does that mean that people with a *growth mindset* don't get frustrated? Absolutely not. Does that mean that they don't experience negative emotions? No. What it means is that after they experience the emotional reaction to the challenge, the success, or the environment, they have the ability to step back and change their perspective. They're able to see the bigger picture and to understand that challenges and competitions – successful or not – are opportunities to grow. They understand that it's not about validating a person's underlying capability, it's about applying a skillset, mindset or talent set. This is critical for mastery of an outcome. Those with an open growth mindset see feedback as a mechanism for growth, and they embody rather than resist the critical nature of coaching.

On the flip side, when coaching a player with a *fixed mindset*, it can make it very difficult and challenging to provide feedback and to train through challenges. We're often placed in a setting or environment in which we're forced to walk on eggshells because we don't want to destroy the athlete's fragile self-image. No matter how hard we want to push, the *fixed mindset* resists, and until the athlete abandons the comfort of fixed, talent-based criteria, continued success will elude them. Remember, a *fixed mindset* comes from a low self-image – EVERY SINGLE TIME. A *fixed-mindset* athlete's mantra is "It's my way or no way," because that's the only way they know how to live.

The Vision for the Future:

As we move through the Game Plan from self-image to internal dialogue to mindset, we see that each of these influences our vision for the future. And the vision for the future is what you really want. It's your passion, the desire burning deep within you. Unfortunately, athletes don't always know what that is, because they're looking so hard for it that they miss the true message.

The vision for the future is either about development or protection. Those who have a positive self-image and who follow the positive self-image pathway of teammate-based self-talk and a growth mindset see the future as a growing vision. They see that their opportunities have not yet been determined, that they're still on the horizon. They understand that potential has no ceiling, and that opportunities are continuous challenges that need to be met.

A great question for someone who has a positive vision for the future is "Where do you see yourself in three months, six months, one year, or two years?" For individuals who have a positive self-image, the answer usually is that they won't be in a much different place than where they are right now, just with some true growth behind them. When you struggle with a vision for the future because you don't inherently believe in who you are and lack the self-confidence to be successful, your vision becomes more about protection and more fear-avoidance. Athletes with this type of mindset and vision for the future generally don't embrace new challenges, because the motivation that drives them isn't to grow through the challenges, but rather to avoid or just survive them.

The greatest coaches I've worked with can build challenges into prosperity. When I'm working with a coach who's had a poor season and is caught up in job security and doesn't see much of a future, I've noticed that he or she almost immediately starts working from a protective vision. On the other hand, when the proverbial shit hits the fan, coaches who have a strong self-image and a great vision for the future understand that they can be the change agent to create the future they want.

When you lose your self-confidence and no longer believe that you're capable of making an impact on those around you, your mind and body go into protection mode instead of continuing to strive for achievement. It's important to understand, then, that your vision for the future has a huge impact on how you build your process and plan.

The Plan:

Let's go back to the scenario of building a house to review the importance of having a plan. As you walk onto a beautiful piece of property, it is critically important that the home be built on a solid foundation. Without a solid foundation, everything built on top of it is at risk, namely because the most important step was overlooked. Likewise, the "land," the environment, and the challenges ahead are always a factor in the plan and process that you're building as an athlete. What are you building toward and how are you going to get there? The best way to properly execute a plan and a process is to give yourself achievable tasks that are challenging and not pie-in-the-sky ideals. A great process and plan is built upon your strengths.

Chick-fil-A, one of the largest fast-food restaurant chains and among the most admired in the corporate culture, doesn't sell cheeseburgers – for a reason. They know what they do, they understand their process and their plan, and they don't vary from it. They work within a model of continuous improvement, and they trust and develop a plan of commitment on a daily basis. They build from their strengths. Chick-fil-A was built on great chicken, served hot and fresh in clean restaurants with outstanding customer service. If you go to a Chick-fil-A in any part of the country, there's a very high probability that they'll be following the same game plan for success each and every day.

It's important that you go through the process and keep track of your progress when developing your plan. Be all in, but review that process appropriately. If you don't write it down, you're not doing yourself any favors, because a plan is obviously only useful when it's followed. Again, it's like building a house – if you don't have a plan, or the plan isn't written down, you're probably going to forget the most important aspects of the process. You'll allow yourself to be guided by the emotion of the moment rather than by the plan, and the biggest traps and obstacles in any plan usually arise in reaction to emotion. These short-term desires to fix the problem and feel relief – rather than sticking to your plan for the long haul and achieving a real feeling of accomplishment – are driven by the low-self-esteem, low-self-confidence model.

Nevertheless, while a great process and plan are best developed around known strengths, most athletes use their practice time to fix problems instead of mastering their strengths. Countless athletes go to the course, the gym, or the field every day in an effort to fix what they consider to be an inherent weakness, driven by the idea that if they just fix that problem, they'll play better. They fall for the fallacy that fixing develops greatness. You have to work on your strengths as well.

Those who struggle with their process and lack a strong self-image usually rely on too many outside sources to be successful. Everyone has a voice, and everyone's voice has meaning, and that's a trap. When you give in and submit to other people, you do what they want you to do rather than staying true to the plan that you developed. People who rely too heavily on advice from others and use yesterday's results to determine today's preparation plan consistently live in a cycle of failure.

Body Language and Interaction with the World:

While the Game Plan highlights the critical importance of a solid self-image and its influence on mindset, vision, and plan, it's also vital to understand how others perceive you. What do other people most often observe about you?

Body language is a factor that has been studied by social and behavioral scientists for years, and it's always interesting to hear the different conclusions that can be reached about how a speaker holds his or her laser pointer. But there really is a lot of merit to the information that can be gleaned from body language. To me, body language serves more as a reflection of what's going on inside a person than it does as a catalyst for that person to change what's going on inside. When I see an athlete exhibiting negative body language as he or she walks around a gym, a court, or a course, I have to be careful not to make assumptions that simply fit my underlying biases. Instead, I try to learn why the body language is being displayed that way. Athletes often don't even realize the kind of body language they're displaying.

One of my early advisors told me a great story about doing psychological work with athletes and how it contrasted with traditional coaching approaches to body language. He said it would be really nice if every time an athlete had a thought, a bubble showed up over their heads and told us exactly what they were thinking. That would definitely make things a lot easier! Unfortunately, none of us has that luxury, so an athlete's interactions with me, the sport, and the team can only be observed through body language, communication style, and other behavior-based displays.

In my opinion, positive body language is most often associated with a strong self-image and a posture that features broad shoulders, a straight back, and the chest held out, as though the athlete's saying, "I have this. I'm in complete control." If we think back to the pilot walking around the airplane before we take off, I don't want someone who's biting their fingernails, slouching their shoulders, and wringing their hands. I want the pilot to display confidence.

Now, are they truly confident? I would hope so, but one thing I do know is that if they don't show confidence, they're more than likely not confident – and I'm getting off the plane!

Athletes who display positive body language tend to make focused, direct eye contact and walk slowly and purposefully, traits that suggest they're in control. It's actually nothing about gait or speed – it's the fact that when they walk, they project an aura of control and the feeling that they can meet any challenge.

When under pressure, most athletes speed up their processes and cognitively tell themselves to slow down. This creates a major internal mismatch that carries through the entire performance spectrum. Positive body language originates from a strong, positive self-image and is influenced by the internal dialogue of a teammate all the way up to a growth mindset and a vision for the future. A positive-body-language athlete has actively engaged in competitive interactions. They want to be in the fight and want to be in the challenge, because they're most comfortable when they're competing.

An athlete with a positive self-image at the core is able to accept responsibility and engage others so that he or she can continue to push harder. It's amazing how an athlete who engages from a positive self-image all the way through their body language can unite a team, and that's why they're often named captain of the team.

On the flip side, as an athlete struggles with self-image, his or her interaction with the world often shows up as negative body language. It's common to see athletes walking around the court or field with slouched shoulders, body language that tells the world, "This is too much for me to handle." These athletes may avoid making eye contact with their coaches and have trouble focusing on feedback, which they interpret as critical rather than constructive. At the core, their self-image isn't strong enough to handle the feedback.

What we often see is fast micro movements, twitching and general discomfort as they move through the environment. Interactions with these types of athletes tend to be all about validation and the search for proof and evidence that early success is important and critical for long-term success: "I need to see success now so I can compete better in the future."

There is one caveat here, and I want to review it. I often get requests from the parents of my athletes to talk to them about their negative body language. As I mentioned before, body language is always a reflection of something deeper inside. So before I talk to an athlete about their body language, I need to understand what's going on beneath the surface. It has been my experience that what parents perceive as a disinterested, disengaged athlete is really quite the opposite. These athletes are often grinding so hard and have become so frustrated that they behaviorally shut down and display little or no emotion, usually because their mind is moving faster and faster in an effort to find a solution. We have to be careful not to make assumptions based solely on body language, because those athletes are often trying their hardest to make things right but lose confidence in themselves. What we see on the outside is body language that's broken down.

Resiliency and Grit:

Body language and that interaction with the world really do influence our road map to success. It's how we engage the world from the outside, but it always comes from our self-image. The most important factor through all challenges is understanding our resiliency and grit. In the past year, psychological researcher Dr. Angela Duckworth has released her book *GRIT: The Power of Passion and Perseverance*[3] and her research findings on resiliency and grit.

While the initial buzz about *Grit*, both the book and the underlying concept, was that it was an all-encompassing panacea and solution to the differences between those who succeed and fail, it is through her research that we've now begun to understand how to overcome challenges through resiliency and grit, two traits that have to be developed. They aren't physical characteristics like the color of your eyes and your hair; instead, according to Dr. Duckworth's explanation through her book, they're skillsets that can be brought out with coaching and through participation in competitive environments.

People with a high resiliency and grit factor usually have a strong self-image. They don't respond to the challenge with an emotional reaction but instead with emotional engagement. The distinction there is that they are engaging with the challenge; they trust their ability to persevere and stick to the challenge rather than looking for an easy out, and they avoid the negative emotions that come with taking the less rigorous path. People with high resiliency and grit simply want to get things done. It doesn't always matter how. The question for them is, can I succeed? They don't care how many scars they have and how many shots they've taken in the battle; all that matters is that they survived and learned something in the process.

These are the athletes who are willing to run *into* the fire rather than away from it, who demonstrate not just emotional engagement but effective problem-solving skills based on the strengths they have and the feats they're capable of. Difficult and challenging environments aren't normally the time and place to try something new (unless that's the only option), but these people are comfortable in the chaos of the moment, primarily because they understand that they sit in the middle of that chaos, that they're part of it. They're always the determining factor in an outcome. They believe, thanks to a solid self-belief model, that they are capable, regardless of the risks, of persevering. Their training has prepared them for this. They may be faced with unknown circumstances and an unknown outcome, but at the end of the day, they're willing to give everything they have, regardless of the outcome.

On the other hand, athletes who demonstrate low resiliency and grit want to do everything they can to escape the outcome. They inherently don't believe in their underlying ability, or feel that they have the self-confidence to succeed. They avoid challenging or competitive situations because they're terrified of being exposed as an impostor or a fraud. Much like people with a low self-image, they avoid challenges at all costs, and their process and plan are specifically designed to do just that. Resiliency and grit are thus never enhanced, because the motivation is to avoid and survive rather than persevere and grow. These individuals tend to quit tasks and activities easily, and they generally lack the self-efficacy to be successful. This puts them at an immediate disadvantage, since we never truly know our ability until we're forced to fight for it. To develop a game plan for success, start with a strong self-image. It is important to learn every day and to see how the growth that you have within you contributes to your self-image. Nobody will do it for you, and nobody will make you stronger. You, as the athlete, hold the key to your own personal success. You'll have very little chance to become more and more successful over time until that self-image is created. It's the only real pathway to success.

Like any game plan in sport, this Game Plan isn't an absolute. It simply highlights the individual perspective of each athlete. There are exceptions, of course, but what isn't an exception is the power of self-belief and the benefits of a solid self-image. From a powerful self-image, the rest of the internal processes are formed in a healthy core, resulting in a better interaction with the outside world. When the self-image is lacking, you're more likely to give power to outside forces. Each of those will be reviewed as part of building your Manifesto, but it is important to appreciate the significance of a healthy self-image. It does not matter how strong the athlete's attributes are, nothing is more dangerous, annoying, and frustrating than someone who lacks self-belief at a core level and undermines those inherent positive attributes. Just because you are an athlete does not mean that your self-image is healthy or adequate.

To build a healthy manifesto, you need to know who you are and the types of challenges that you face. The Game Plan lays out how the interconnected psychological concepts impact you and your competitive environment, but the only way to improve is to work at the core. Each of the factors discussed in the following chapters work at the self-image level. It is the most important level to work from, in the core center of who you are deep inside.

6

The Power of the Athlete/Person Dynamic

I work with people. People compete in sports and become athletes. Athletes learn from their time spent in the sport and apply it back to life. Those athletes once again become people. It is the cycle of human development through sports.

What makes sports so powerful is that there are new challenges and opportunities to grow every day. Remember: As people, we're always striving for something, and sports provide that avenue. Life can also be so complex and difficult at times that sports become an escape.

Understanding success and failure in sports is often more about understanding the challenges that we face and the intricate aspects of the human personality. We are complex creatures, but for no greater reason than our ability to choose our approach and our mindset, and for our ability to flow through emotions.

One of the first sports clients I ever had the pleasure of working with demonstrated that beautifully. He was a young high school golfer who, like a lot of athletes, placed significant pressure on himself to succeed. His parents were very supportive and were careful not to place athletic or academic pressures on him. Any pressure he felt was self-inflicted; he was simply eager to equal or surpass the achievements of those in his peer group who he felt were enjoying increasing amounts of success.

Early in his junior year, he won a very large and prestigious tournament. The field was full of the best of the best, but he won easily. Almost immediately, he began to change. The "normal" amount of pressure he had experienced to that point suddenly increased to paralyzing levels. He was desperate to be recruited by the best colleges in the region, and he believed that this victory would turn the coaches his way and he would have the pick of the teams.

Unfortunately, every round of golf he played after that victory was painful. His emotions had been heightened, and his expectations were off the charts. With every shot that failed to meet his "What college coaches want" standards, he became increasingly frustrated and angry with the game. It got so bad that one well-meaning coach suggested to him that he should just have fun and not get so emotional out on the course. This, unfortunately, just made things worse. Now, in addition to the pressure of just competing and playing his best in each tournament, he was trying to impress coaches, play for fun, and not get emotional. It was a recipe for disaster.

When he contacted me for my services, I was impressed with his ability. For a player his age, he had a tremendous ability to swing the golf club, and he was also a very pleasant and enjoyable conversationalist. He had tremendous knowledge and awareness of current events, and he regularly and fluidly interjected references to historical figures to describe his own feelings. He was also very insightful about his current situation and what he thought might be contributing to the struggles in his game.

As we discussed his circumstances over the next few weeks, he began to reveal more and more about himself. As it turns out, he didn't really want to play college golf. What he wanted was to have that option and to be respected for his game. Deep down, he wanted to go to law school and invest heavily in his academic career. Golf was always enjoyable until he won that tournament. At that point, he lost control of his emotions, allowed his expectations to rise, and changed his mindset.

As it happened, that was our last appointment, and I honestly thought I had failed as a sports psychologist. Here was a super-talented golfer who was walking away from the game when others in his situation were starting to really make that college push. Deep down, I worried that being a sports psychologist wasn't for me, just as being a collegiate golfer wasn't for him.

Six months later, after high school graduation, I received a voice mail from his mom. She wanted to meet. I was nervous and really dreading the meeting. I was sure she was going to tell me that she was disappointed in the outcome of our sessions, and that I had failed her son.

But when I walked into a local coffee shop for our meeting, she got up and gave me a huge hug. She actually had tears in her eyes. She went on to tell me that she was extremely thankful for the work I had done with her son. He was a different child – he no longer walked around the house in anger, frustration, and depression. She told me that when the pressures of golf were removed from the equation, she had gotten her son back. I agreed with her, but I also reminded her that the game had probably taught him some valuable skills and awareness, that he had learned how to make positive choices – possibly for the rest of his life – manage his expectations, and better understand himself. Sports, with his blessing, had provided a valuable environment for learning.

This young man is now attending a very prestigious law school in the Southeast. He has a plan, he's happy, and he still plays golf – with his friends on the weekend. We ran into each other recently, and I asked him what the biggest change had been. He told me that he had been playing golf for the wrong reasons – he wanted others to accept him. Yes, he wanted to succeed, but being admired as a great golfer by his peers was more important than anything else. As a result, his expectations rose, his emotions ran wild, and his enjoyment of the game quickly disappeared. His name will always be on the trophy from that tournament, but now he sees it as a positive and not a burden.

For the most part, we can't control our emotions or our thoughts. Emotions make us what we are. They are the lifeblood of the human experience, and our ability to arise from anger, happiness, jealousy, love, pride, and other emotions each day is what primes our ability to connect to our pursuits. Without emotions, there would be no connection. Our young golfer didn't choose to put too much pressure on himself, but he did choose to continue to do so once he had started. Let me explain.

This young man initially wanted to play at the next level in college, and that's where he set his goals. As his expectations rose, however, he began to experience thoughts that he was not succeeding, which increased the emotion of frustration. By continuing in this fashion he believed he was doing the right thing, but he was actually just choosing to continue the maladaptive patterns of high expectations and volatile emotions.

When I say we can't control thoughts, I'm merely referring to the fact that the human mind is an amazing filter of information. Throughout the course of an average day, when pressure and intensity are low, the mind allows thoughts to pass through the consciousness. These thoughts pop up in your mind all day long, usually without any real meaning or the need for you to take any action. They may be silly, constructive, or destructive.

Now, it's important to understand that in pressure situations, this process typically changes. Pressure circumstances like the end of a basketball game, an important putt, or a fourth-quarter drive increase the volume of thoughts.

Think of it this way. You have an amazing new surround system in your living room. It has nine speakers pointed at the seating area, and behind the seats sits a powerful subwoofer. Like anyone who's spent all that money for a new surround audio system, you have to get a movie that has large explosions, displaced sound, and loud noises. If you set the sound at 20/100 on the dial, the integrity of the sound will be fairly good. But all viewing rooms have an optimal range for the highest integrity of sound, and as you push the dial up, you'll quickly notice that increased volume eventually overtakes the fidelity of the sound. As you approach the 80/ or 90/100 level, the crispness of the sound succumbs to the power of the noise, and the resulting cacophony overwhelms your senses (and ears).

When the stereo sound gets too high, most people make the choice to turn it down. Athletes can do this too. The "sound" of pressure in a competitive environment simply increases the clutter and the number of thoughts running through your mind. More and more thoughts – mostly counterproductive – begin to pop into your head. What you choose to give power to in your thoughts will stick around, and then actually start influencing your emotions. So the goal is to put an increasing amount of space or time between the thought and the emotion you feel. You can do this first by understanding that your thoughts have no power unless you give them power, and second, by lowering the volume – that is, by bringing the pressure down.

This takes awareness and, most importantly, a conscious choice. While you may not be able to change your thoughts, you can choose to change your overall mindset and perspective to influence how you react to those thoughts. By changing your mindset and perspective, you can attend to other, more important thoughts, which in turn allows other consistent thoughts to flow in. In other words, it is like flagging e-mails.

When you check your e-mail inbox, you'll usually find e-mails that have been read and others that are listed as unread. The mind will be drawn to the contrast between those two categories, and depending on the number left to read, your stress and anxiety can increase. If you're feeling overwhelmed by work and feel pressured on time, the increasing number of e-mails in the unread box just serves to reinforce how much more you have to do. That pressure, however, may not be beneficial – it may be hard to filter the remaining e-mails to read for high-importance subjects and identify those previously read to complete tasks. To improve productivity, you have an option to flag e-mails, which helps draw your attention to those messages that require additional attention so you can consciously pull them out from the crowd. Completing those tasks raises productivity and reduces the amount of work left to complete.

When your awareness and mindset are focused on growing, competing, and learning, your thoughts will run with more of that kind of synchronicity. But when you're lost in a flood of pressure conflicts, your thoughts will group together in negativity, resulting in immediate emotional frustration. As you get more frustrated, your thoughts collect negativity like the lint screen in your dryer. However, you can choose which thoughts you want to give power and attention to, so give it to the productive thoughts.

We all wake up every day with a choice: to live fully or to allow life to live us. Choosing to embrace life means that you're making an active choice to live with the potential and greatness that you embody and the opportunities that are out there, and that you understand that challenges are simply opportunities to learn more about yourself. Every day, you choose to embrace the challenge of sport and to engage in the process of improvement. But it will never just happen to you. You have the ticket, but you have to use that ticket to get into the arena. Ultimately, you choose between the things that allow you to grow and the things that are stunting your growth. You can't change the thoughts, you can't control the world around you, and you can't change your past, but you can always choose how you respond to life. Choose wisely.

Expectations and pressures can be both good and dangerous. It's how you choose to look at them that defines their influence and importance to you. Expectations are entitlements – they're pressures that you place on yourself and that arise from things you've done in the past, such as successes and failures; the need to validate your effort and intensity of practice; and the hopes you have of changing the course of your performance. Expectations are ultimately driven by fear and doubt and fueled by hope. But none of those are good. All expectations will do is raise your emotional state to one of heightened pressure and overwhelm your God-given ability to compete.

So should you have expectations? Not if they're going to increase pressure. All great athletes and teams have a vision for what they want. They're not rudderless in the sea of competition. They have a vision, but they don't *expect* it to happen. They fight for it, work for it, and adjust to make it happen. When expectations are high, the outcomes become about what "should happen." But there are no "shoulds." In other words, nothing is ever guaranteed – *nothing.*

You have to know who you are and what you embody. That always trumps expectations. If you're emotional, be emotional – but don't judge it. Emotions are great if you express them naturally. When expectations are high, emotions are usually only expressed in a self-destructive way-judgmental, impatient, and unrealistic.

Why would you squash excitement? If you nail the game-winning shot, make a huge putt, or hit a home run, the natural reaction is to be excited. Allow yourself to experience that emotion. When things are good and you're not faced with adverse pressure, you can refocus your mind on the next play, the next shot, or the next experience. As expectations and pressure rise, the negative thoughts that flood the mind trigger what behavioral scientists call "secondary emotions." (Plutchik, 2001). Essentially, these are a layer removed from the natural emotional experience and are typically directed at you – getting angry about getting angry; expressing frustration for hitting a bad shot because you continue to do so; getting worried that you're worried about a game. Secondary emotions, fueled by expectations, ramp up the experience in destructive ways – it becomes pure self-criticism. Why invite an opponent into your head during competition? That's basically what you're doing when you allow emotions to take over.

Getting angry is normal, but continuing to pile on secondary emotions is a choice. The decision to continue to be self-critical happens because there are no defenses against such personal attacks. While it may feel productive at first to get on your own case, it doesn't benefit you in the long run. Your emotions are allowing you to continue to attack the only true champion: you.

Instead of watching the secondary emotions run wild and provide a fertile ground for high expectations, it's important to understand that emotions are good for you, thoughts are natural, and nervousness, pressure, and intensity are simply part of the competitive equation. It's important that you choose to see the game and competition differently.

Physiologically, discomfort, nerves, and adrenaline are the same thing. At least initially. They all enhance arousal. So the bigger question is, what are the feelings and emotions telling you? It's common to strive for perfection and become over-analytical. But you have to let things foster growth and create opportunity for success. The internal feelings you feel aren't wrong or bad. They're just feelings. They're not emotions until you label them. For example, if you're standing outside a room and the locked doors prevent you from entering, and you realize that your heart is racing, you're sick to your stomach, and you have sweaty palms and can't stand still, which emotions do you think would immediately come to mind? Nerves and fear?

You may be completely right. It's easy to create a scenario, for example, in which a meeting about whether you were going to keep your job or not was being held behind the locked doors. But what if the discussion behind those closed doors was actually to determine whether or not you were going to be awarded a multimillion-dollar raise? With nothing to lose in that scenario, I'm sure there would be a few nerves, but the real emotion would be excitement. Same physical and psychological feelings, right? But different emotions. It is all about how the individual appraises the situation that determines the emotion of the moment.

Think of it as a person you don't like showing up at a party you're attending. Are you going to confront them, or are you going accept the fact that they're there and simply decide not to let their presence ruin the party for you? The response to that question depends on the person being asked, and there's never a right or wrong answer. But emotions are sensitive to the environment, and they can tell us when it's important to address a situation and when it's better to just let it go.

You're human, an imperfect person who is working as hard as possible to learn more about yourself through competitive experiences. From a competition standpoint, you need to know what ultimate intangible you possess that can help you succeed. That's your advantage, and it's how you can use your emotions, decisions, thoughts, and pressure to work for you rather against you.

It's what I call The Competitive Magic. [See next page]

The left circle describes the area in which so many athletes function. In that circle are all the things under your control. Whether it's how you practice, how you eat, or how you receive your coaching, the circle is essentially your preparation plan. In theory, the harder you work, the bigger, stronger, and more powerful that circle becomes. On the right is your goal: success. The desire to win and to continue to win is the goal of most, if not all, athletes.

A common misconception of generations of athletes is that if you do everything you can in the left circle, it will lead to success in the right circle. That may be a great story, but it's not really accurate. The greatest athletes in the world embody something else: They have the "IT Factor." The best of the best understand that *they* are the ultimate intangible that brings all the factors under their control and allows them to use those factors to compete for the ultimate outcome. The factors in the left circle are the investments and the outcome is the profit, but the IT Factor – you – is the vehicle that makes that happen. And it never happens without the IT Factor.

Those with a great IT Factor understand that there will be times when their emotions are out of control and others when their emotions are in check, and times when the game is easy and times when the game is hard. But regardless of the circumstances, they are essentially still the same person.

High-achievers who embody the IT Factor understand what they want and are ready to do what it takes in competition to get there. They keep their expectations down but the demands on their process high, always scrutinizing the situation to see how they can make the process work better for them. Each game, match, or event is a learning environment. It is never determined. These high-achievers are willing

COMPETITIVE
magic⟳

MANY ATHLETES BELIEVE THAT CONTROLLING
WHAT THEY CAN CONTROL WILL LEAD TO SUCCESS

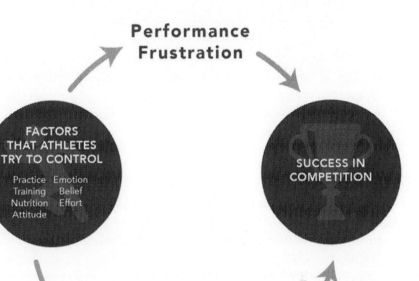

**Performance
Frustration**

FACTORS
THAT ATHLETES
TRY TO CONTROL

Practice Emotion
Training   Belief
Nutrition Effort
Attitude

SUCCESS IN
COMPETITION

the
IT
factor

TO BE SUCCESSFUL

Great Competitors take
their investments & use their
IT factor intangibles to win.

to sacrifice a lot to reach the pinnacle of success, but they're also able to sacrifice one thing that few others are willing to give up: their self-preservation aspect, often referred to as the ego.

The greats just see the game differently, and I think it's that gap between training and success that makes them better and better. It's hard for an athlete to let go of the training circle. But does this mean that training isn't important? No. In fact, exactly the opposite is true.

Training is the investment that you make in yourself and your process to achieve success. It's how you apply it – understanding your emotions, limiting your expectations, and choosing to persevere through the uncertainty of life and sports. The investment is deposited each and every day during training, put away for withdrawal when it's needed. Unfortunately, too many athletes fail to invest in themselves, and when competition gets hard, the only thing they can do is borrow against themselves, paying interest and hoping that they can get the competition loan. What is it that they are borrowing? Hope. When athletes fail to invest in themselves, the only thing that they can rely on in high-pressure environments is hope that they will be able to find something to succeed. The problem is that this is not a sustainable performance model.

Great athletes think differently. They know they have the investment in the bank, and they trust that they can draw on it when it matters the most. It's not about finding magic, it's about trusting in those investments. It's the difference between hoping and knowing. Furthermore, the greats know that they themselves are the sole factor that differentiates them and their competitive mindset from those hoping to find it each game or week.

I've never met a champion who didn't believe in his or her ability to compete. When they are open and honest about it, it always comes back to the IT Factor, something that they believe about themselves that helps them overcome the challenges and win. Knowing that you embody a secret that your opponents may be lacking is incredibly empowering. And if it's so powerful and effective, why not learn to develop one for yourself?

7

The Drives of Life

One of the universal questions in sports and performance psychology revolves around the passion that a coach and a player possess. When you wake up in the morning with that drive, that yearning to achieve something, everyone can sense it. What's even more noticeable, however, is a person who's living life without a purpose or a connection to their desires.

You weren't born with some random, undetermined navigation plan, one that's only influenced by the shifting wind on any given day. If that were the case, success would simply be a matter of luck. It is definitely more than that. Deep down lie passions and drives that guide your journey through life, both at home and on the field. They are unmistakable and universal in all human beings.

Throughout my work as a clinical psychologist, and now as someone who works in the sports and performance world, this has always been evident. We're all propelled forward by a series of drives that guide, motivate, and sometimes even inspire us to reach for more. The passion that wakes up with us in the morning is the same passion that climbs into bed with us, exhausted, every single night.

This book is not about finding that passion. I don't believe you find passion; I believe that passion finds you. When I was struggling to find my purpose long ago, my mom told me not to look for a career but for a job. It's through working a variety of jobs that your career will find you, if you open your heart and mind to it. For me, that was sage advice. I went into clinical psychology and training through graduate school with the idea that I was going to work in private, clinical settings. I had all the ideas, especially coming from the business school, where I had sharpened my inherent entrepreneurial spirit. Upon completion of graduate school and an internship, I turned down a prestigious post-graduate fellowship at one of the top hospitals in the country. Why? Because I knew deep down that it wasn't my passion. I decided instead to take a job in research and development with a Northeast pharmaceutical company. It was a dramatic shift for a clinical psychologist who was still wet behind the ears, but true to my mother's advice, it was a job, not a career.

After roughly eighteen months in that position, I was ready for a change. I was bored and tired of being stuck behind a desk. I hadn't yet gone through my licensing process as a psychologist, and honestly, I wasn't sure I wanted to do it. I was attracted instead to the busy and energetic world of business development, and I felt that it might be a great transition. I took a job with another pharmaceutical company, but this time as a medical liaison, where I developed research, collaborated with the business units, and helped drive innovation. At the time, I really felt that I was moving toward something resembling a career. Turns out, however, that it was merely another job – the excitement lasted for a few years, but then I found myself getting restless again.

Looking back, the transition to my current role was set in motion many, many years earlier. When I entered graduate school, my goal deep down was to be a clinical and sports psychologist, but I was scared to death to admit it, work for it, and sacrifice for it. I searched for sparks, I searched for solutions, and I searched for escape routes that would all lead me to my passion. I had an amazing boss and team at the pharmaceutical company, and while I might bemoan the travel and the demands of the job, that was really more of an excuse rather than the true source of my discontent. I was lost because I was disconnected from the Drives of Life.

For me, it was clear: I was lacking the reinforcement and excitement that accomplishment and achievement provide. It was hard to go to work every day just for the spirit of work. As a former collegiate athlete who had played on numerous championship teams, accomplishment and achievement were the culture, not the goal. If you weren't making progress in your role or your path, someone else was coming for your job. It wasn't personal, just reality. Championships were demanded. Passion was lived daily.

I struggled to find that again after school. Although I was making a very nice living – significantly more than many of my graduate psychology colleagues, and even more than my mentors in the field – I wanted more. I wanted the risk, the sacrifice, and the passion that came with fighting for something. I desired more simply because I was living without a goalpost. It wasn't about the money, or the job title. My passion was dying, and that scared me to death. It scared me so much that I almost just took another job, which would have been devastating for me and my family. Thankfully, a conversation with my wife and parents changed my perspective. They demanded that I have patience, that I allow my desire to build, that I tackle the ups and downs that are inherent to any kind of success in a way that my family could handle. The job was safe, so we would build toward the dream without pulling the safety net. Keep the passion, but keep the backup plan a little longer.

They were right. I could find my passion without risking my family's financial security and way of life – for now. Not long after accepting that, I was asked by a local coach to answer some questions that he and one of his players had. They both wanted to know how he could better coach through some difficulties that the player was facing at that time. It was a fairly innocent question, but it ignited a powerful spark. I started to help that player on the side, free of charge, and before long that player became two players, and then three, and then five, and then even more coaches. The next thing I knew, I had to start charging for my time. It didn't happen overnight, but it wasn't a particularly long process, either. Eventually, I grew this side business to a point where I simply couldn't keep it at bay anymore. The success that my players were now enjoying had become something of a tidal wave (although, as they say, "Great players make a great coach, not the other way around," so a lot of the attention I was getting was due to the fact that I happened to have some great players). But I was hooked, and the factor that was lost in me for so long was no longer lost – I was feeling the competition and that drive for accomplishment returning. It was like a drug for me. I stayed awake at night, thinking of ways to be a better coach, a better communicator, and a better ally for my players. Never once did I think about marketing – only improving my approach, perspective, and style.

There is nothing better than being in the hunt for a win or a championship, or building a team with players and coaches. Your passion becomes clear. It's always evolving, because your needs and drives evolve. But what never changes are the drives themselves. We're all driven by the same things — it's universal, but few understand it and even fewer respect it. These drives are what pushes each of us through the ambiguities of life and human performance.

The Three Drives of Life

1.   **The Drive for Accomplishment:**

Why do you get up and moving each day? Is it simply to exist, or is it to get things done, work toward a goal, or overcome a challenge?

Few people truly live just to exist. Those who do are simply passed over by people working to achieve outcomes.

We all have a drive deep down inside. It is a yearning, a purpose, a calling. We spend hours reading interviews with the greats simply to garner some insight into what makes them tick. What drives these people? Where have we gone wrong?
Why do we even have a calling, when the truth is to simply survive this crazy world?

Life and competition are hard. If there were no outcome to work toward, we'd end up walking in circles, tripping over the footprints we made three minutes ago. Our vision and perspective would be focused on our feet, not on where we were going. The mind is driven by where we are going.

We're all driven to accomplish things. You can say it doesn't matter, but it always does. Think about the times in your life when you were the most focused and engaged — it was about doing something, never about avoiding anything. We're all driven to accomplish something. It could be a puzzle. It could be getting a job interview. It could be losing weight. But the brain, the physiological organ in our skull, is driven by accomplishment, and so too is the mind, the often-discussed center of conscious and subconscious experiences. Life isn't just about existing – it's about rallying our resources to fight for success and to push for achievements and their benefits.

But to go a bit deeper, even accomplishment isn't really the goal. Higher-level learning is the ability to put together a plan of action, to find a process, to gain an accomplishment. But without a vision in mind, and even more the deep drive to accomplish, we would never even lay out the plans. That's the ultimate goal.

And that's why most overnight successes lack the connection – it was too easy and there wasn't a process in place. In real rags-to-riches stories, there's always a process – fueled by a passion to achieve – behind the scenes. It's a combination that drives all success. Unfortunately, when the process is lacking but achievement is desired, the door is opened for shortcuts and other easy fixes that short-circuit the system. Athletes do this all the time, whether that means using performance-enhancing drugs or seeking out other inappropriate competitive advantages. Success and the desire to achieve it are always about the process, and that commitment usually only shows up in the long run. Any benefits achieved through shortcuts rarely last.

The larger problem is that we as people – and more so, as athletes – get bored. The accomplishments of today are never enough to feed the hunger of tomorrow. We want more and more, and so we set new sights. Reaching a goal is an addictive experience – it floods the brain with a series of neurochemical changes and an excitement and hunger to achieve more. With that rush sometimes comes the misconception that all accomplishments are easy, but in the immediate short-term, it always looks great. I always find it interesting when celebrities branch out into other industries – we've all seen, for example, musicians who want to act or athletes who want to play in a band. Why would these people want to start over and go through all the sacrifices that it takes to succeed when they've already succeeded in a dramatic way? It has to be that need to accomplish something important. Many celebrities and athletes have been focused for so long on their goals and their dreams that once those have been achieved, the competitive nature that got these men and women to the top in the first place immediately shifts to a new challenge. There is a calling, a yearning, to succeed with all they have. Yes, their status makes things a bit easier, but effort is still required. And for most of these people, the competitive drive to succeed is alone enough to overcome the challenges inherently present in any activity.

Accomplishment, achievement, and the processes implemented in their pursuit are core to the human experience. Through the journey to achievement, the pathway to mastery is always revealed.

When we lack the connection to accomplishment, the boredom and absence of purpose create a deep void in our psyche at levels far beyond what is observed. The drive to push through the process when the going gets hard is an easy antidote for boredom and the lack of a purpose. But it's important to understand the challenges and consequences faced by a person whose purpose isn't engaged – these can include a lack of direction, a lack of initiative, and a lack of resiliency, among others. When things reach this point, the only solution that may be readily apparent to the frustrated competitor is to simply stop trying to achieve, accept the victim role, and try to pass the blame for one's difficulties to others.

As an athlete, the accomplishments I'm talking about are rarely the large, high-profile victories that we're all so used to reading about. Rather, the victories and accomplishments to which I'm referring are the little ones – the daily wins and the daily commitment to follow a process that allows us to realize our potential. That's the real accomplishment toward which we're all driven.

2.   **The Drive for Social Acceptance**

We are social creatures. We all want approval and acceptance from our friends and colleagues. That's why we want to drive nice cars, dress nicely (at least some of us), and constantly compare ourselves to others.

At all levels of life, social acceptance and the ultimate need to connect with our colleagues on an emotional level define our actions. You may think that it's only in high school where defined social constructs and cliques become reality (and, often, painfully exclusive), but everything we do in life and sport involves the power of social acceptance. In both of these arenas, we compare ourselves to those who are – or who are perceived to be – slightly higher on the social ladder. We want to be liked and valued. On the flipside, the comparisons also involve those with a lower perceived social status, but the motivation is different. In this scenario, it is about avoiding the group that we are trying to break away from or avoid regressing back into. Very simply, we run in groups and strive to run in groups that we desire.

Humans are driven at a core level to find connection and support from those around us. But as we'll discuss later in the book, when that desire for connection and validation from others comes at our own expense, we lose our ability to succeed.

Social media is a perfect example of this inherent need. From Twitter to Instagram, the power of a simple "like" can be tremendously influential on our future actions, so much so that our decisions are often guided by our ability to collect more likes and make ever-wider social connections. In the advertising world, advertisers measure the ability of the contracted celebrity and the depth of the celebrity's personality on the social connection to their followers, simply to determine if product investors can quantify their results by leveraging that social connection to sell products. At the core of that is the need for social acceptance.

As soon as we find comfort and satisfaction with our current social group, that group is changed. We then identify a new group, and our behavior shifts in an effort to gain acceptance with that newer group. We never seem satisfied until we run out of groups to break into.

We may be in a constant battle to be accepted, but social groups change. Think about the hottest club in town. One week, it's the best place for dinner and drinks – it's *the* place to be seen. Give it a week or two, however, and that "hot spot" will be re-created somewhere else. The members of the flock simply follow the other members to the next hot spot, but no one really seems to know why they're in the flock, other than that's where everyone else is.

Athletes are not immune to this, but the motivation may be different than club-goers. Many pros simply want to "make it", but after "making it" some shift their vision to becoming an all-star. Very few shift their desires to becoming a hall of famer, but those that do continually set sub-goals to reach their desires. This progression is not for everyone as only those that are willing to sacrifice everything can reach the ultimate levels of success. Those that are willing to make those sacrifices are those that are willing to shift their mindset for greater challenges.

For junior athletes, the desire to be recruited by area colleges falls right into this paradigm. Deep down, every athlete wants every coach to be clamoring for his or her services. But when the athlete is on the outside, the need for social acceptance rears it ugly head. This negatively shifts their level of performance because the athlete becomes concerned with their performance equaling a college scholarship, rather than competing in the present challenge. It is an amazingly predictable trap that often has tough consequences.

In my opinion, isolation is the fastest way to crush a person's spirit. The adverse impact of social isolation has been well documented in numerous studies of prisoners of war. Prison inmates are subjected to long periods of solitary confinement and it's clear that a lack of regular personal connection and communication can be simply devastating to the human psyche. Remove a person's social reinforcements and connections and you can singlehandedly break that person down.

The need for social acceptability is really a matter of finding peace with those around you. It is not until you realize that the futile efforts and negative impact of chasing approval are robbing you of your true ability, and as a result, the only way to maximize social acceptance is to invest in your own performance as opposed to what it means.

Social acceptance is also about social respect. We want others to know what we've gone through to succeed, and being accepted by a group that you strive to be valued by only reinforces the idea that you've persevered just like they have. (The old saying that "misery loves company" also applies here.) In every endeavor in life and sports, human beings want to be connected to those who have walked the same paths, climbed the same stairways, and jumped the same fences.

3.   **The Drive for Stability**

Human beings also yearn for predictability and stability. We don't function well in unstable conditions, or more accurately, we don't *think* we function well in unstable conditions. We actually work very well in chaotic situations, but we still yearn for stability. In all of our interactions and engagements, we want to get to the point where we see predictable results. Unfortunately, once we get that, we often create chaos, usually by disrupting the stability with the drive for more accomplishment or the drive for more acceptance.

But it's true – we function very well in chaos. In fact, chaos – as we'll discuss in the chapter on focus – is the norm, not the exception. The forces that work against chaos are predictability and stability, so when life and sport become difficult, stability looks very inviting. And it's that desire that motivates us to find a new coach, or read new material, or examine each and every facet of our games – these are all attempts to create consistency and stability.

I like to think of our brains and minds as those kitschy snow globes sold in airport bookstores. With the snow resting softly on the ground, the scene is tranquil and picturesque. But with a flick of the wrist, the water-filled globe is suddenly turned into a raging blizzard. Little pieces of imitation snow fly everywhere, continually pushed around by the current. Only after a time does stability return – the water quiets and the snow settles to the bottom of the globe. You can't speed this process up.

Life can be the same way. Our snow globes are often turned upside down. Our lives swirl, our minds spin, and the world seems to move faster and faster around us. Our senses become overwhelmed, and we yearn for stability. We're not always patient enough to let life settle back down on its own, however, and the harder we try to influence the process, the worse things get. Simply accepting the fact that the snow is going to float around chaotically for a while will go much further than curling up on the ground and crying that the water isn't clear. Accepting whatever stability you can find within the chaos is a choice.

Ultimately, stability comes from the chaos, not in spite of it. The longer we enjoy stability, the closer we get to turning it upside down and starting again. It is a matter of time, not a sign of weakness. It is a sign of humanity. In fact, the more chaos there is, the more that becomes the norm, and that actually becomes stability. It may sound strange to think of it that way, but the contrast in the moment is often where anxiety arises from.

Let me explain in a bit more detail. Too many people get so caught up in worrying about the next potentially negative event that they find it impossible to live in the current moment. It's as though the uncertainty of the future means more to them than the living breathing experience they're having right now. The reason for this is that the present moment, regardless of how much chaos is going on, is actually a known commodity – it's stable. It's easy and common for us to accept and minimize the known moment because while we want stability, chaos is easier to embrace as a standard. And yet, conversely, when we're in the middle of chaos, stability is craved.

Gaining stability in life and sport is about understanding what causes stress and what brings comfort. Learning to identify the sources of your stress – even if they happen to be things that you think you enjoy – can help with the stability process. It's not about eliminating things from your life, but rather, it's about understanding the impact that those things have on you. It's about moderation and buffering the impact.

The power of stability comes from the fight for it. Stability is truly ingrained by the daily effort to eliminate stress and to appreciate the predictability of the factors that make you a better person. We all want that, regardless of our background, belief system, or comfort zone.

To be successful, you have to know what drives you. But when you use one drive to fulfill another drive, you lose balance in life. Success and accomplishment cannot create stability in the long-term. Each drive must be invested in independently. One cannot ever fulfill the drive of another. Only when you value each drive for its own purpose can the stability of the human psychological drive take over. The game is hard enough that stacking the drives against you will only cause more problems. In order to be successful, you need to understand how each drive impacts you and how your internal motivations are aligning to gain success.

8

Learning is Part of the Process - The Pathway to Mastery

S everal years ago, a young high school golfer's parents and coach asked me to work with him. The player was very talented, but he was struggling to succeed in bigger tournaments. His parents were prominent in the community, and a lot of attention had been focused on the young man.

I worked with him for nearly three months on his process and his mental approach to competition. In high-profile tournaments, he placed a huge amount of pressure on his performance and on what a high finish would mean in the college recruiting process. He would play well in the opening rounds, then consistently struggle as the fields got smaller. He was understandably frustrated, and his parents seemed even more frustrated than he was. Not a healthy combination.

I felt that he had made significant progress as we worked together, although that progress may not have been particularly evident to someone on the outside. I stressed to him the importance of implementing a strategy before each round that was consistent with his preparation plan leading into the tournament, and told him that when he felt stress, he should rely on the aspects of his process that had been put in place for such situations. He really seemed to resonate with the instruction — or so I thought.

One day, I got a blistering e-mail followed by a blistering voice message from his father. He apparently felt that his son hadn't improved at the rate he felt he should have, and he was therefore discontinuing my services. I contacted the player, who told me that his dad felt he needed to figure things out on his own. Not bad advice, actually – just poorly delivered. And disappointing to me.

After I recovered from my own frustration at not having been able to help this player faster, I reflected on our work together in an effort to figure out how I could be a better coach in the future. I had been pleased with his progress, although I felt he needed several tournaments over the next several months to really learn how to compete under pressure. Because he was more talented than the average high school golfer, many of the beneficial processes that should have been part of his training regimen weren't in place, and his practice habits were random and inconsistent. The truth of the matter was that up to this point in his golf career, his talent had overcome his many deficiencies. But now that the talent level of his competitors had equaled or surpassed his own, he had begun to struggle. I felt that my plan was a very good coaching strategy, and despite a few minor tweaks here and there, I was satisfied that there wasn't much I would have done differently.

I went about my business and tried not to take it personally. Then, about a week later, a funny thing happened. I received a message from the player, who told me that he'd had won a very prestigious junior tour event. He was very excited and thanked me for our work. I definitely appreciated that, but what was even better was that he went on to win the next two events, which gave him three victories in a row and much-needed affirmation of his ability as a player. He was so excited, and I was very proud, because I knew the work he had put in for three months had contributed to his success. He had learned how to compete, and he also told me that because I had always impressed upon him the need to "figure it out" for himself and to learn from each event, he had begun to come up with his own solutions during matches using the information he had prepared. Bingo!

A few years later, the player's father called and asked me to work with his son again. The young man was now a college golfer, and being the glutton for punishment that I am, I agreed to help him out. To be honest, my decision wasn't that hard, because this kid was a fantastic person – humble, appreciative, and responsible. Over the next two months, we worked hard on some of the same processes and factors that had led to his earlier success. In his next three collegiate events, he showed remarkable improvement, recording a top 10, a top 5, and a third well-managed tournament. He was playing with confidence, and he appeared to have figured out his pathway to success.

Amazingly, I then received another e-mail and voice message. I had been fired again! Based solely on a less successful fourth tournament, the father felt that his son was still struggling and had lost his confidence, and that our work had essentially been a waste of money. All I could do was shake my head. That was probably the absolute worst time that his son and I could have stopped working together, and I let him know that. But he was adamant – he thought it was time for his son to start relying on his team of coaches and to work on his own to find the secret that would carry him through bad tournaments. He had made up his mind, and that was that.

This young man had been learning all along, but unfortunately, his father was measuring his performance strictly by the low points. The problem with that is that the low points are normally where a player learns a lot. By abandoning the plan when he did, the father was putting the continued growth and success of his son's golf career at risk.

Each athlete has to run the peaks and valleys of human performance. It happens every single time. "Nothing comes easy" is a great saying that we've heard for years and years, and for a good reason – there's a lot of truth to it. Challenges and difficulties have to be overcome if one expects to grow.

When I'm working with clients, I always find that when they come into my office, they have preconceived notions about the learning process. One of those is that things will get worse before they get better. But nothing could be further from the truth. Learning is the building block of what we are. It's what we experience every single day. If we don't learn, we don't grow. If we don't grow, we don't gain new experiences.

Learning is the key to everything, and it's important to understand how the cycle of learning truly happens when an athlete is going through changes or learning a new process or technique. When an athlete begins working with a new coach, or starts working on something completely new, there are a couple of motivations that tend to influence the overall outcome.

The first, from the athlete's perspective, is the desire to fix the underlying problem. This is a trap. Trying to fix a problem is different than trying to master a sport, a position, or a movement. The idea of trying to fix something is rooted in anxiety, and when anxiety is the motivational factor, our struggle simply becomes an attempt to overcome that anxiety. The goal is no longer success. At that point, the goal is nothing more than survival.

The Honeymoon Effect and The Crash:

When an athlete says, "I want to get better" or "I want to improve," I want to know why. Do they want more consistency? Do they want to improve? Do they see an opportunity? That's the start. When new material is presented, they quickly begin to experience what's known as the "honeymoon stage." This is a great place. The coach and athlete are able to simplify the process and the overall understanding of what they're going through. At that moment, things are fresh and new, and the clutter of past difficulties is swept away. Overthinking has been replaced by focused intent, and at this point, the athlete normally feels better, more excited, and more engaged in the process. The honeymoon effect is very powerful, and it keeps you motivated as you try to make changes, but it only lasts for so long.

As an athlete continues to enjoy the burst of enthusiasm associated with the honeymoon effect, they begin to believe that they can do almost anything. They start to believe that they've got it figured out, but that's usually the point at which they start to turn their attention away from continuous improvement and onto expectations and perceived outcomes. This is where the crash begins. They move their focus away from the simplicity of their actions and overcomplicate their process. What seemed easy during the honeymoon effect is no longer easy. What had become simple is now simple with additional information, and that additional information clouds the mind, clutters the intent, and slows down the motor process. This crash has happened to every single athlete I have ever worked with.

It's how they manage the crash that makes the difference.

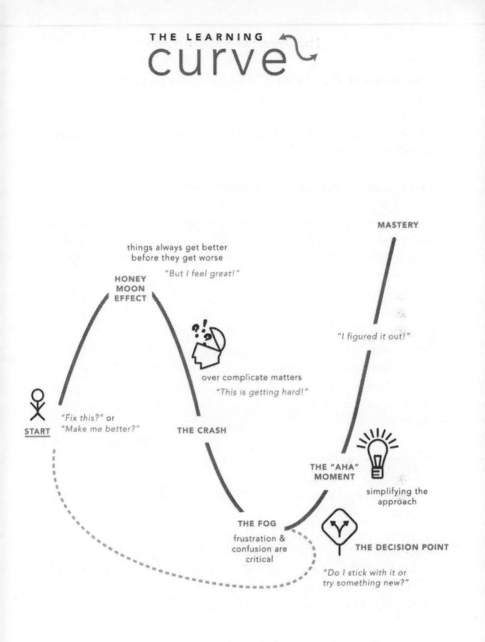

The Fog and The Decision Point:

After the crash, these athletes move into "the fog stage." The fog is a dangerous place. It's a place of frustration and confusion. When athletes enter the fog, they usually start to call their coaches in a panic – they've forgotten everything that they ever learned, their frustration levels are going through the roof, and they want to abandon the process and the plan that was created for them. (Of course, that process is what allowed the athlete to enjoy the honeymoon effect in the first place.) The fog is where everything that you once thought was easy is now hard. The simple is hard, and the hard is impossible. Once in the fog, the athlete has to make a choice, which will determine whether he or she gains mastery or falls back into the cycle – the choice to stick with it or abandon the plan and find a new fix.

The performance fog isn't much different than driving in a real fog. When you're faced with foggy conditions on the road, you don't use your bright lights, you turn the radio down, you turn any inside lights off, and you slow down. You have to reduce internal and external stimuli and then focus on one or two points on the road that will allow you to successfully navigate the clutter and distractions that can enter your field of vision in this weather. Learning a new process in the game of life and learning one in the sporting world aren't much different. You have to slow down when you're in a performance fog and recognize that frustration and confusion are natural, not indications of a failure on your part.

Frustration and confusion have to be in place if you expect to move on to mastery. If you haven't gotten frustrated and confused as you try to learn a new approach, you probably aren't trying hard enough. The challenge isn't great enough. Frustration and confusion commonly arise from a deep doubt on an athlete's part about his or her ability, and chances are good that you have similar doubts. When you get frustrated with your progress, try to figure out what's behind your frustration. Is it belief or doubt?

In order to move from the decision point and exit the fog, you need to be committed to, and have belief in, the process you created – the same process that was responsible for the honeymoon effect. When this happens, you'll be able to move on to the "Aha Moment." There's nothing better than an athlete experiencing success and mastery by working through the challenge (and the self-discovery that goes with conquering a challenge) themselves. Self-discovery – which is the ability to find a pathway through the skillsets you already have with the help of trial and error and experimentation – is a powerful but often overlooked learning tool.

The Aha Moment and Mastery:

When athletes train in structured settings without the opportunity for self-discovery, they are robbing their own inherent ability to learn and master a skill. The "Aha Moment" comes when, in the middle of the fog, you're able to quiet down your internal stimuli and focus on the most important components of your success. When that light bulb goes on, that learning skill is never forgotten, and it moves the athlete to mastery. I've worked with client after client on this cycle, and while I'd love it if athletes didn't have to suffer through frustration and confusion, it simply has to happen. The difference between going through this experience as a coach and dealing with it as an athlete is that coaches generally understand that the confusion and frustration are simply vehicles on the path to mastery, not destinations.

The emotions that drive frustration and confusion are often different than the emotions of mastery, but you have to learn how to manage all of these individual emotions, and put them in check, in order to move on. It's never easy. No one ever said it would be. To learn how to be successful is to learn how to manage the fears, the doubts, and the insecurities that are with you every step of the way on the learning curve. If it were easy, you wouldn't learn.

Think back to math class, when your teacher presented with you a new mathematical equation and a new strategy on the board. At first, it's probably a little confusing, but then a light bulb goes off. You can see the solution very easily, and with each example that the teacher presents, you begin to feel more and more certain that you've got the concept down. That night, while you're doing your homework, you start to work on some of the problems. The first few are easy, often almost literal interpretations and executions of the mathematical formulas you studied in class. But over time, the examples get harder. What was easy is no longer so simple. You start to doubt yourself. The problem is, if you look to somebody on the outside to give you the answer, you'll miss it. You have to find the answer inside, and this is exactly how a good teacher imparts knowledge to his students. You show them and lead them but allow them to find the answer themselves. It's just like math – when you work through the struggles and the difficulties, and finally come up with the answer and can see how the dots connect, you'll never forget how to do the problem.

This happens with athletes all the time. They'll often struggle early in their careers, but as they gain knowledge and expertise over the years, they become increasingly more successful. They've learned how to eliminate clutter in the learning process, and because they struggled and experienced frustration and confusion, now know how to distance themselves from the idea that they – as athletes and people – have somehow failed. It's not about them anymore. It's now about the solution, and about doing whatever it takes to get things done and to succeed. Self-discovery is often the vehicle needed to work through the learning curve.

Beyond the learning cycle, performance gains follow a formula – they grow then recede, grow then recede. And here's the crazy thing – when they recede, they actually do so to a level that's below the last surge point. Learning and seeing improvements is a long journey. If you spend your time looking at the individual data points, it becomes so difficult to stay on track. The individual ups and downs take the emotion right to the forefront, where it fights for and against the struggles and successes. It's vitally important to understand that the overall process, not the individual data points, is the goal.

I see it all the time with athletes. We start to build a plan designed to help them succeed. They're very often at or near rock bottom when we get started. If I were to ask what success meant to them at that point, they might mention improvements or seeing those improvements on a daily basis. But once they start to actually see improvements, their perspective changes, and so does the appraisal and their emotions.

What happens is that we push the baseline up and we push the success line down the road. Nothing is ever good enough. So as we move along the improvement roller coaster, we start at a foundational baseline and over time surge to a peak, which then, for a variety of reasons, starts to plateau and then regress. Now, while the regression may not take us back to rock bottom, it can actually feel like that, because it goes deeper and further than the last foundation at which we started.

But the truth is that the improvement foundation is now higher than it was before – it just feels as though it's harder. Expectations change, and expectations are performance killers. That period of frustration and confusion about why you've regressed is necessary for long-term success. It hurts in the short term, but it's critical for long-term growth. Unfortunately, those same athletes who jump off the learning curve as soon as it gets hard panic as their struggles increase.

It takes significant trust in the process to know that when you recede, the next growth is actually going to be better than it was before.

But that's the point of the experience – it gives you the ability to accept that you're in that position, you're making overall improvements, and that by managing your process and daily pursuits, you'll be able to work through it. Athletes who start at rock bottom often react negatively to this process because they're scared to death that rock bottom is the new normal, when in fact it's just a transitional starting spot.

Instead of thinking about the future, think about where you are today. Is it good or bad? Why does the mind seem to default to bad? The key to success is acceptance – the ability to look in the mirror and accept what you are today, and to realize that while your current situation may not be ideal or where you ultimately want to be, just fighting and competing is good enough.

Acceptance is one of the hardest things that human beings have to face, because it means that we can no longer anchor our mind in the future of what we want to become, that we have to look and be aware of what we are and how we plan to compete with what we have in the present.

Unfortunately, athletes often build themselves up to be the ideal warriors that they're certain they'll become. Of course, this is usually not based on any facts or evidence, just on hope and expectations. When reality sets in and it doesn't meet their expectations, they'll usually get frustrated, instead of recognizing that what they actually have is damn good enough.

Remember, frustration and confusion are a necessary part of the learning process. Too many people, athletes included, try to navigate this process without having to face hardship or struggle. The fact is, if their motivation is to fix an issue and not master a movement or skillset, learning becomes a tremendous battle. Parents unknowingly do this all the time when they search for easy ways to alleviate the pain and discomfort that their children (and all children) inevitably face in life. It's important to understand that frustration and confusion are part of the journey, and that the best medicine is to persevere with a plan.

Learning is life. It is simply part of the process. No one is ever judged on the championship medal stand by their lack of scars. No boxing commentator has ever said that the heavyweight champion of the world is less of a champion because he suffered a bloody nose and a swollen face at the hands of the opponent he had just defeated. A champion learns from every landed punch and uses that information against his opponent. Champions are heralded for their ability to learn and adapt to the challenges of competition.

9

Managing the Mental Burden

S uccess comes with a great burden. Simply succeeding once is never the goal – it must be done again and again. Once an athlete reaches a desired level of success, the bar is raised almost immediately. The responsibility to continually live up to new, more challenging expectations and pressures can be difficult, but for great athletes and teams, that burden isn't resisted or avoided. It is embraced.

On my way to work recently, I listened to a press conference with Nick Saban, the head football coach at the University of Alabama, in which he discussed the mentality behind the Crimson Tide's success on the gridiron. "During a game, the outcome, on average, comes down to six to twelve plays," he said. "Over the course of a hundred plays, these six to twelve – which are unknown, can't be predicted, and often arise out of unique circumstances – completely change the course of the game." Since the college football season is relatively short compared to those of other sports, and since one loss can make or break a school's chance for a national championship, those six to twelve plays can literally mean the difference between having a successful or a lost season. If that's the case, why would any player at any time have a mental letdown that would increase the odds of one opponent or another defeating you on those plays?

The point that Coach Saban was trying to make was how important it is for players to stay mentally locked-in and focused for every play of every game. As far as Coach Saban and his Alabama players are concerned, the team's on-field performance should be a perfect reflection of Saban's practice philosophy and preparation program, which includes nutrition, strength and conditioning, human psychology, and a businesslike approach to winning.

By understanding the flex points of their games, and having their players mentally engaged on each and every play, Saban and his staff increase the team's odds of success. During the game, the difference between players who are mentally engaged and those who are taking the play off can mean the difference between a linebacker grabbing or missing the leg of a runner, or a defensive back jumping in front of a pass for an interception or just knocking the ball down. Fans and commentators often miss what the coaches see: the ability of a player to make a play when no one is prepared for it – in other words, one of those six to twelve plays that can change the entire course of a game and a season. Needless to say, every player on the Alabama roster appreciates the importance of being mentally ready.

The greatest challenge facing any athlete is staying mentally focused and engaged during each and every competition and training session. This is much easier in competitions against your crosstown rival or other high-adrenaline games. Maintaining that same level of intensity and engagement when you're playing a team or an athlete that you should beat, however, is more difficult. If you're not mentally engaged and ready to compete, those "easy" games can quickly go south.

The mental burden of sports is significant, and over the course of a long season, athletes must deal with the ups and the downs and the physical and mental exhaustion that wears on them every day. This is why professional athletes generally train year-round and college athletes train for nearly ten months a year. They all need their minds to be ready and fresh when the schedule starts to become a grind. The beginning of the season is easy – the mind is engaged, excited, adrenalized, and ready to compete. Can the same be said at six weeks, or three months? Probably not. Those who train to improve not just their physical fitness but also their ability to stay mentally locked in and focused every week can only increase the odds of their success.

It is important for athletes to understand the things that actually drain their mental energy so that they can not only get rid of those distractions, but can learn how to build up their defenses against them. Not all distractions can be removed; in these cases, the athlete must learn how to create a buffer against them. Some of the distractions in an athlete's environment include personal demands, athletic demands, physical demands, fears, doubts, and insecurities, all of which can sap the athlete of the mental energy needed to be successful. What ultimately wears an athlete down, however, is the burden and expectation of great play, not the activity itself. This is important. If you're competing in a difficult game against a crosstown rival who has equal or better talent, it's generally accepted that the game's going to be a battle. Likewise, if you're a golfer who's playing a difficult course in a big event, you know the tournament's going to be tough and that every round will require the total involvement of all your senses. There's little doubt that at the end of each round, game, or match, you're going to be mentally exhausted. Of course, having given it your all, that's what you want to be.

The above doesn't describe the mental burden, however. The mental burden develops when we fail to pay enough attention to the little things in our preparation and our execution. Over time, this neglect starts to suck the energy away, because we're forced to rally all of our resources just to stay above water, let alone succeed. Let's focus first on the field or in-competition mental burdens.

The number-one mental burden faced by athletes is **high expectations**. Expectations are entitlements. They are driven by fears and doubts, and use past experiences to create hope for future outcomes. Most athletes raise their expectations when they're struggling, because they're hoping beyond hope for an outcome that will quickly turn around their sagging fortunes. As they continue to struggle, they raise their expectations higher and higher, but when their performance inevitably doesn't meet their expectations and reality comes crashing in on them, pure mental anguish takes over.

The expectation gap between reality and belief is what creates this divide. Athletes feel let down and frustrated when reality doesn't meet their expectations. That doesn't mean that an athlete shouldn't have high demands and goals – quite the opposite. To counter unrealistic expectations, athletes must approach their training sessions and competitive events with purpose, mental engagement, intent, and a specific plan for every play, set, or shot. They must also resist the temptation to guarantee an outcome or result.

Using these demands and goals can help mute expectations, and this is when athletes tend to play great. It's also why an athlete who is sick or hurt often plays well – he or she simply has no expectations. They allow the mind to do what it's trained to do without trying to overcontrol it or protect it against a negative outcome.

Another mental burden is the **fear of failure** or **the fear of success**. When we're terrified of an outcome because of what it may mean to us or the burden it will require us to carry, we're no longer competing in the moment. Instead, we're competing for validation of the meaning *behind* the moment. That creates a tremendous amount of mental anguish, because the competition itself requires every available mental resource we have, and if we play for something other than the competition itself, those resources are diverted and wasted.

When we're trying to prevent the fear of failure, we're actually trying to prevent a reflection of who and what we are. This is why athletes often become perfectionists – they feel the need to control everything they can to ensure success. But it goes even deeper than that. Perfectionist athletes are trying to avoid becoming what they fear in themselves, and this creates less than an ideal competitive mindset. That's a shame, because if an athlete can allow himself or herself to be vulnerable to the outcomes, he or she will be secure in the knowledge that even if they're not successful, they'll be fine. It may not be the ideal outcome, but they'll survive. In the end, fear of failure and fear of success are significant mental burdens simply because they involve an attempt to control an outcome. As we've stated numerous times, this is something that human beings just can't do.

The third most significant mental burden that athletes face is having a **letdown against inferior competition**, or inferior athletic demands. Coaches fear playing down to their competition. Athletes often see lesser competition, a field that's not as deep as it could be, or a weaker team, as a place to coast. The problem is, in the middle of the coasting, the opponent, the field, or the course fights back. With nothing to lose, they play above their ability. Now we have a team that's playing down to the competition and another that's playing up, and suddenly, the nominally more talented athletes are scrambling to rally every resource they can to overcome the threat. The burden of competition isn't the issue – it's the burden of dealing with the expectations and a possible letdown, not to mention that having to unexpectedly tap every resource at your disposal empties the mental energy bank. It's better to approach every game with a clear idea of what you want to learn about yourself, rather than simply trying to achieve a particular outcome. Competition is a myth – if you're mentally engaged to compete every time, the competition you face won't raise or lower your ability.

The distractions and demands of competition can have a lasting impact. If, over the course of a season, you lose a little bit of mental energy every day, you simply won't have the ability to give 100 percent of what you've trained for when the end of the round, or the end of the tournament, or the end of the season rolls around. You'll be functioning at a reduced percentage of your full energy potential, and unfortunately, you may not even notice it until it's too late.

On-the-field distractions aren't the only mental burdens. Like the rest of us, athletes have to deal with personal issues – relationships, family matters, contracts, or the countless other problems that life sends our way. Demands from family members and friends often distract an athlete from his or her ability to focus on the task at hand. Professional athletes, for example, are often required to entertain out-of-town friends and family. This may be great for the visitors – who are on vacation and understandably enjoy watching someone they know compete – but that's not usually the case for the athlete, who's trying to do his or her job.

Can you imagine friends and family asking a neurosurgeon to go out for dinner and stay out until midnight the night before a major early-morning surgery? They'd be taken to task for such behavior. But athletes who have to make split-second decisions and maintain intense focus – so that they can perform at an extremely high level and continue to make a living – are often expected by friends and family to entertain and be socially available. The athlete must learn to put up boundaries and raise defenses against these external threats and demands. You're not being disrespectful by putting up boundaries, you're just helping your friends and family understand what the rules of engagement have to be. My experience is that the overwhelming majority of friends and family want to do what's best for the athlete. But more often than not, the athlete is reluctant to let the family and friends know.

Other external demands include contracts, media status, and college recruiting. Let's talk about that last issue for a minute. For a high school athlete, junior year is usually one of the most stressful periods of their scholastic career. College recruiting and commitments are in full swing, and athletes invariably get caught up in which coach is in attendance, which coach is offering their competitors, and how many spots are left to fill. Athletes need to understand that the college recruiting process is ultimately out of their control, that there's very little they can do off the field to influence it. The only thing a potential college athlete should be focused on is what he or she can control, and when. College recruiting is often a mystery, and it's vitally important for an athlete to remember that every game, every round, or every tournament they play in isn't a matter of life or death. If they compete and work hard, they'll most like have an opportunity somewhere at the end of their career. It may take outside-the-box thinking – such as trying to get an academic scholarship or making a team as a walk-on – but these strategies have worked for many, many athletes over the years.

When mental burdens rise, the mind suffers – it goes into overdrive and recruits every available resource it can to survive. It shifts the mind away from thriving, and to succeed, athletes must be in a thrive mode, not a survive mode. These mental burdens challenge even the greatest athletes in the world, but it's the athletes who can eliminate distractions and protect their own psychological well-being over the course of a long season who tend to stick around. That's why professional athletes have begun to invest in proper sleep hygiene, nutritional counseling, and recovery rehabilitation – they understand that many factors once considered to be solely part of the physical realm can actually offer tremendous mental benefits. So they commit every day to making small choices – such as going to bed fifteen minutes earlier, eating a healthier diet, or getting off their feet and stimulating blood flow – that will give them an edge.

An investment in your mental wellness has many long-term benefits. It allows you to stay in the moment and avoid predictions, high expectations, and other psychological stress – you're awake and mentally alert, and you're able to focus exclusively on making the plays and executing the strategies that you've worked on in training. When athletes invest in their mental wellness and remove the burdens that drain their mental and emotional energy, they often go on to become championship players who can manage a much greater variety of demands. But whether it's the expectations that come with a large contract, the pressure of playing in front of 100,000 fans, or just the stress involved with making a varsity high school team, distractions and demands put every athlete at every level at risk. So it's important to invest in improving your wellness. Make the small choices every day that will improve your mental and emotional well-being, so that when you need to draw on the energy resources necessary to meet the demands of the game, they'll be there.

10

The Pressure Moment - Employing
the Switch

The U.S. Navy SEALs are considered by many to be the most elite military fighting force in the world, and they and their training programs have been profiled extensively in articles, movies, books, and documentaries. To become a SEAL, candidates must successfully complete a physically and mentally demanding six-month training program known as BUDS (Basic Underwater Demolition/SEAL), which is conducted outside San Diego, California.[4]

The BUDS program is divided into three phases, and is designed to train and select the strongest men in the force based not on their performance at a single task, but for their ability to endure for the duration of the program. At any time during training, candidates can quit simply by ringing a bell at the training site three times and leaving their helmet in a line of other candidates who have chosen to leave training. With a nearly 80 percent failure rate, SEAL training is obviously not for those with doubts, but instead for those who desire to succeed more than their doubts would seem to allow.

The climax of the BUDS challenge occurs near the end of the first phase, commonly referred to as Hell Week. While the first phase is generally focused on the physical and mental conditioning of the candidates, Hell Week is designed to significantly intensify the training over a five-day period. Candidates average about four hours of sleep – for the whole week.

The challenge of Hell Week is to maintain one's mental focus on the task at hand instead of becoming overwhelmed by the amount of training still to come. For those candidates who complete Hell Week, nearly four months of training still remains, so to successfully endure the physical demands and sleep deprivation requires an immense amount of focus on the present.

Successful completion of BUDS also requires a mindset that values excellence in the basics rather than superiority in a limited number of extraordinary tasks. Every BUDS candidate has been tested and screened long before arriving on the beaches for training, and all are in excellent physical condition. But BUDS training combines the physical and the mental. It requires, for example, the ability to run and swim long distances and endure extended periods of time in cold ocean water while still focusing on the mental challenges of the "evolution," a term used to describe a particular segment of the program.

The ability to run long distances for time – over and over again, on the beach, while wearing combat boots and covered head to toe in sand – requires different mental and physical skills than those needed to swim two miles for time in the open ocean water against the current, or those needed to sit in freezing water, locked arm and arm with your teammates as the waves crash through you and onto the beach. (Not to mention, of course, the skills needed to shoot with precision, jump out of high-altitude airplanes, navigate underwater vehicles, or disarm underwater detonation devices, all requirements of the BUDS program.) With each task and in each evolution, attention to detail is emphasized and is critical for success.

SEALs who complete BUDS then participate in a series of other training programs, and only then are they ready for assignment to a SEAL team and eventual deployment around the world. Although the SEALs originated as a maritime force, their level of training and expertise in a variety of situations has made them the group of choice to resolve conflicts and execute high-profile missions anywhere on the planet, even when the closest body of water is hundreds of miles away. SEALs training prepares these men for the most intense, pressure-packed environments imaginable – everything from direct combat to diplomatic negotiations.

And even though BUDS eventually ends, training is never really over for a SEAL. Once assigned to an individual SEAL team, SEALs continue to train for the rest of their career. And it's not simply about rehearsing – the physical and mental demands are continually increased over time. This is the kind of mindset that separates SEALs from other people.

Of course, every branch of the military uses intense programs to train its soldiers, pilots, and other personnel, and highlighting the SEALs in no way implies that the other branches aren't as prepared. It's just that the nature and purpose of SEALs training is different. These men and women train for the unknown, the uncertain, and the chaotic, and the style and intensity of their training reflects that.

Chad Metcalf is a former Navy SEAL who has had a number of combat and diplomatic deployments around the world in his twelve years of service. After high school, the Texas native was working at a community golf course when the terrorist attacks of 9/11/01 changed the course of his life. A high school golfer who had entertained thoughts of playing in college and professionally, he felt a larger calling to serve his country after 9/11. He was actually turned away by the Marines because of an old arm surgery, but he returned nearly two years later to sign up for the SEALs, determined to test himself in the most difficult training program in the military. Metcalf completed BUDS on the first attempt, and he shared his thoughts with me on success he's achieved through the training and continued development as a SEAL.

Metcalf highlighted a few important points that outline the best way to succeed under pressure as an athlete, business leader, or, in his case, someone who's transitioning to a career as a professional golfer. These help demonstrate what it takes to succeed when the chaos of the moment increases or the pressure of competition intensifies, and they're part of what I like to call The Switch (more on that shortly):

1. **Rising Up to the Moment is an Illusion:**

    As a Navy SEAL, you don't rise up to the magical moment of a challenge or transform into a super warrior simply because you're in an intense conflict. Instead, you fall back on your lowest level of training when the crucial moment arrives. The high-profile heroic actions of the Navy SEALs (and servicemen and women in other military branches, as well) have been well documented, and it's a common belief that these actions demonstrate unreal levels of bravery and courage. It's true that Metcalf has served with a Medal of Honor recipient and numerous others who have displayed unreal acts of bravery in the face of significant threat to life, and there's no doubt that he's experienced that level of intensity himself. But he maintains that all of those heroic acts were based on training, and that they were implemented by people with an intense will to execute at their level of expertise. It wasn't a matter of someone trying something new or finding a completely new source of insight. He admits that he's been immensely humbled by the bravery and valor of some of those actions, but he still makes it clear where it all comes from: training. In the world of the Navy SEAL, each and every circumstance is trained for – there's a plan A, a plan B, and so on. SEALs train for their worst day, not their best, so in the chaos of combat, they can trust that they've trained themselves well enough to adjust to the demands of the moment. Without this training, the complexity and adversity that they've faced would have quickly exposed holes in their readiness and implementation. SEALs execute at the level of their training, not with the help of some mythical ability.

2. Train to Prepare for the Unknown:

Training is about simulation, not elimination. During training exercises, Navy SEALs spend endless resources, both financial and psychological, to replicate any environment that they might possibly encounter. For training to be as realistic as possible, SEALs build exact replicas of buildings and villages to fully simulate planned operations, and during these simulations, they work through every possible scenario – positive and negative – that the mission might hand them. SEALs train in chaos so that they can naturally transition into a competitive or combat mindset. By raising the level of intensity in training, SEALs and their leadership try to re-create every possible situation, so that when a plan goes awry, the challenge can be responded to with a deep understanding of what needs to be done. Thinking, per se, isn't necessary.

3.   Failure Must be a Part of Everything:

In training, every outcome has a consequence. ALWAYS. SEALs are inherently competitive, but that competitive nature is raised to a new level in BUDS. The reason is simple: competitiveness in training and life is a trait that can be drawn on when a plan or mission is being executed. For SEALs, every training operation is either a competition between groups or a challenge in which a poorly performing team can be punished. That doesn't mean that the SEAL team trains to avoid punishment rather than to master a task. It just means that because there are real-life consequences in combat, there have to be similar consequences in training. When shortcuts or bad habits are introduced into training (these are referred to as "training scars"), they will invariably raise their ugly heads in high-intensity situations. If a SEAL were to decide that he or she was going to take a break and loaf during a training operation because it "doesn't matter right now," that diminished level of execution will show up when it matters the most – and risk the lives of all involved. Without consequences in training, it's easier to take shortcuts and just assume that the proper reaction will be there when needed. The easy mentality is to endure rather than master.

The Navy SEALs are masters of execution. They train under pressure to execute under pressure. Spending time with Metcalf and other SEALs showed me that the level of intensity of their training represents a culture of excellence, and that through failure and mastery, they're prepared for any eventuality.

I get referrals every week from parents and coaches who want to understand how their athletes can play better under pressure, and more importantly, how their athletes can take what they learn in practice and transfer it to the playing field. Most players work very hard in practice to understand exactly what they're supposed to do in a game, but things are completely different once the actual competition begins.

What do we know about competition? First, the environment of a competition is a much more variable. Let me explain. In a game, pretty much everything is unknown. The only things that we're sure of are the rules and the time. That's about it. Conversely, in practice, you can control just about any factor that you choose. You can take away control, and you can give control. You dictate the environment. As a coach, you can set up an intrasquad game, or you can have your players run a drill and try to overcome a challenge that you've created.

As a coach or a player, you can do your utmost to mimic a highly competitive environment, but it's never quite the same as the real thing. In a game, pressure is just different. The variable nature of competition almost always increases the amount of pressure on the players, because they're now competing against someone or something that really doesn't want to give up any control. In golf, for example, every shot you hit is from a different lie and a different yardage, and with a variety of clubs. Every play you call in football and every shot you take in a basketball game has different circumstances surrounding it.

It's important to understand the difference between how the mind functions in practice and how it works in competition. In practice, we commonly try to improve and build, and to do this successfully, we know that we need to give up some of our ego attachment to outcomes and results. We also know that when we try to improve, we're likely to fail more than a few times along the way.

Competition, however, is different. In an actual game or match, you're battling for an outcome, for something that you desire and something that means a lot to you and the people around you. This means that every play, every shot, and every outcome has a significance that's much deeper than just improvement.

This creates a huge pressure burden on every athlete on the field. When I evaluate athletes and work to help them improve their games, I often make use of examples from other industries. One of my roommates in college is now a trauma orthopedic surgeon. I asked him how he handles pressure. I found his answer to be quite interesting and something that all athletes can relate to and learn from. As a trauma orthopedic surgeon, he said, you never know what's coming through the door, except for one thing: You know that the individual on whom you're about to operate has been involved in a traumatic event and needs medical attention.

You may have certain pieces of the person's medical condition and history, but that's about it. This means that the surgeon has to do a rapid and immediate assessment to figure out exactly what the next move should be. Thankfully, he or she understands that there are components and factors that they can control and procedures that they can fall back on every time, regardless of the situation's particulars. Whether it's breathing, circulation, or any other system, they understand the factors that are at the core of everything they need to do regardless of how the pressure may build – and it does build. People talk faster, think more intensely, and act more purposefully. The role of the trauma surgeon is to constantly exhibit control, even if control isn't yet a given. Whatever's happening around them, they need to maintain a demeanor that says, "I'm in control."

Athletics is no different. Whether you're playing in Yankee Stadium, or at the U.S. Open, or in your backyard, or at a local municipal course, the golf course is the golf course, and the ball yard is the ball yard. Nothing changes except how you embrace and engage the pressure situation.

If, like a lot of people, you find that you succeed in practice but struggle in competition, there are a couple of steps you can learn to make the cognitive adjustment to the challenge at hand, managing the increased pressure of competition, or what I call The Switch. Before going into the individual steps, it is important to clarify what I mean as The Switch – The Switch is the mental switch that happens in athletes that actively engage the challenge of the moment and competition and embrace the uncertainty. It is only then that they become comfortable in the uncomfortable, and become masters of the competitive moment. The Switch is the mental operation behind the physical experience of competition, and the steps to make **The Switch** are:

1. **Abandon the need for validation and ultimately embrace the challenge of competition.** To abandon the need for validation, you have to give up the need for approval and acceptance from your coaches, your family, and your friends.

Competition demands everything from you. If you take some of that competitive power away by trying to please a coach, a scout, or college recruiter, you're giving up control and power and using precious resources to deal with a distraction.

2. **Learn to accept the fact that the outcome is always uncertain, and instead invest in the process to achieve a desired outcome.** The results of every game you play are unknown. You simply can't control outcomes. Most people try to control outcomes because they're trying to prevent a negative outcome, as though they're not capable of handling the bad as well as the good.

What does it say about you if you can't handle the negative? It says that you don't have faith in yourself to manage both the good and the bad, that you don't have the ability and the resources to overcome challenges, and that if something is going to go your way, it must go perfectly. To make The Switch in competition, you have to accept that the outcome is unknown but be willing to fight for whatever happens with everything you have. Investing in the process is the way to get there.

As reviewed in an earlier chapter, athletes with the IT Factor can take that process and that training and the things under their control and do something with them to help raise the probability that they'll achieve an outcome they desire. Let's be real. If you're competing and you're not trying to win, you might as well stop going to competitions. We compete to win. It's who we are. One of the underlying drives is accomplishment. In order to be competitive, you must let go of the need to control the outcome but invest everything you have in trying to achieve the outcome that you desire.

3. **Compete with a present focus.** The single most important question you can ask yourself is, "What is important now?" If you don't play to get your coach's approval and validation, and you don't play for the outcome of the game so that it can give you that validation, you can then play with a present focus: "I accept the things I've done in the past. I know the future is uncertain,

but the only thing that matters is now. If I've won every match before this one, this match doesn't know the difference. I must meet the demands of this match right here, right now, with all of my resources aligned to reach that goal."

It's a simple question, but it's hard. Most human beings are desperate to rewrite the past. If we've had troubles, we want to make them better – not for the present, but to make the past more accommodating to our mindset and our ego. The future is unknown. We have to accept that. Every moment and every second is a blessing. Nothing is a given. If we can't control the future, and we can't rewrite the past, why not invest in the present?

In order to make The Switch, the game that's right here and right now – regardless of your past successes and failures, regardless of the decisions that are going to be made and the opportunities you're going to have in the future – is all that matters. The moment is now. Those who can make the cognitive switch to be great in competition are the ones who can focus on the now-the present moment and challenge.

4. **Use tools creatively.** It's how you apply them that really matters. Imagine that you've hired a carpenter to move a wall and install new windows in your house. Do you want a carpenter who only has one tool? What if that carpenter attended just one weekend workshop and only learned how to use a hammer. As the old saying goes, if all you have is a hammer, everything becomes a nail.

What makes the master carpenter brilliant is that he or she can take any tool in their toolbox and use it not only for what it was intended for, but for a wide variety of other functions. Good craftsmen learn to use tools to do whatever they need to do to get the job done. They aren't limited to a tool's stated or primary purpose.

I see this with athletes all the time. They get stuck trying to apply a strategy or a technique in a strictly literal sense. They don't allow themselves the cognitive and physical flexibility to apply the tools they have in new ways. Just because you use trial and error and get creative doesn't mean that you're abandoning what you've learned. You're just looking for alternate options and thinking outside the box, because if you don't, you're going to be very limited when you try to apply your training. An athlete becomes a creative artist when he or she can take the skills they've learned and apply them in a unique way to handle whatever situation or challenge they've encountered. That's what it takes to make The Switch.

From understanding how US Navy SEALs prepare for The Switch in an unknown world to the athlete preparing for competition, it is important to explore the traps and challenges in everyday experiences that make it difficult to execute The Switch. In order to fully understand the types of traps and their impact, it is critical to understand the differences between practice and competition.

What is the goal of practice?

To learn the skills necessary to compete. To understand routines, processes, and activities that are repeated over and over until they're ingrained. The goal of practice is to "overlearn" technical skills so that they become second nature in in competition. That's great. That's the goal. There's nothing wrong with that.

You also identify weaknesses and work to strengthen them, and identify strengths and make them even better. That's the goal of practice. Your focus during practice, however, is different. Your focus there should be on accepting the fact that you're in a controlled environment and that getting better is a process that you put in place through the use of systematic training and experimentation, and that allows you to continue to improve slowly and steadily over time.

Because you have more opportunities in practice, you can repeat a drill or a skill until you get it right. Failure is inherently normal in practice. In fact, failure in practice helps identify weaknesses. Your focus on failure may be different in practice. Your focus on failure suggests that it can be corrected by continuing to work at the skill and that when you do fail; it's simply part of the process. But through success and failure, your focus during practice should be on your internal processes, on HOW you do things. That's important, because when we make the switch to competition, our goals and our focuses change.

What is the goal of competition?

To compete without compromise, hesitation, or fear. To lay everything on the line, give it everything you've got, and to leave the playing field mentally and physically exhausted. If you're not exhausted when you leave a competition, you haven't given enough. Now, of course, there are the rare, magical circumstances where the game is so easy that it doesn't tax you mentally and physically, referred to as the "flow state" or "zone" by Mihaly Csikszentmihalyi in his book *Flow: The Secret to Happiness*.[5] But otherwise, competition *should* be exhausting. (For a more exhaustive review of flow, I highly recommend Dr. Csikszentmihalyi's book and *The Rise of Superman: Decoding the Science of Optimal Human Performance*[6] by Steven Kotler).

If you're holding back, ask yourself why. Is it to protect yourself, to protect your self-image, to protect what other people think about you? If so, all you're doing is building up angst, anxiety, and stress, which will create more exhaustion in the human body. Why not try to leave everything on the line and give it everything you've got? The true athlete who can make The Switch is the one who leaves nothing behind and can walk off the field, the court, or the course safe in the knowledge that regardless of outcome, they gave it everything they had each and every time.

The goal of competition is also to apply your skills in your own adaptive way. Let's use golf as an example. You can practice using a lob wedge to chip around the green over and over again until your hands are sore. But in competition, can you look at a situation that requires that exact shot – only this time, from an uncertain lie to an uncertain pin – and creatively figure out how to get the ball close? You can't control the situation. It's unknown, and although you may be familiar with the shot from practice, you've never seen it set up exactly this way before. Can you meet the demands, or – like a lot of junior golfers I've watched – are you going to step back and say, "I don't know how to hit that shot" and just give up on the challenge?

Those who can compete will look at the situation and say, "I'm not supposed to do this really well. But I've never seen this before, so I have nothing to lose. Let's give it a shot." Those players are the ones who are the most creative and the most successful over time. One of the goals of competition is to understand how to physically and psychologically adjust to changing and unfamiliar environments. This uncertainty and ambiguity is what makes great competition fantastic.

You may think you know what a game is going to be like, but it very rarely goes according to script. The athletes who can make the cognitive switch to be fully engaged in competition and to compete without fear of outcome are the athletes who see tough demands and uncertainties as part of a fun and challenging environment, not a stressful, invalidating environment.

And finally, let's be honest: The goal of competition is to win. Why else would we do it? If you're not trying to win, why are you doing this? For a participation medal? Come on. You're better than that. Winning is fun. Winning and the success of accomplishment are part of the core nature of who we are as humans. We are competitive beings.

It is a reinforcing model. You want to win. You push harder. You push harder, and you win – and then you want to win some more. This is why Las Vegas uses bells, whistles, and every psychological ploy in the book to trick their casino customers into believing they can win. They know that the desire to win is what motivates most of the people who walk through that casino door. And there's nothing wrong with winning or trying to win, as long as you do it in a safe and predictable manner and with respect for your competition.

The focus of competition is to understand that the competitive environment is variable and uncertain. The challenge is how to meet those demands. Your focus should become external in competition – to see what you want to do and how you want to do it, rather than just if you can do it or to prove to yourself HOW to do it. See where you're going to hit the shot, or where you're going to make the pass. As Wayne Gretzky, the greatest hockey player ever, once said, "Don't skate to where the puck is, skate to where the puck is going."

Those who effectively employ the cognitive switch always see ahead because their focus throughout the competition is external – they trust their preparation and their internal processes to create the outcome they desire in the external environment. They're not seeking external validation for their internal processes. In fact, they are doing the exact opposite. They are a trying to create and perform in the external environment.

An elite competitive focus is understanding that resiliency and uncertainty, and being able to manage the ups and the downs and the frustrations and the excitement, are what lead to competitive mastery. Being frustrated during competition is normal. Competition is never new, the environment may be an unknown, but the competitive environment of heightened arousal and the battle of the moment is never new. Those who can manage the cognitive demands of competition usually succeed, because when they do get frustrated, they know that it's not an ultimate outcome, just an emotional pathway on the way to the destination. These are the athletes who consistently employ the cognitive switch in competition.

Elite athletes and Navy SEALs embody many of these same attributes, and the focus of SEAL training can serve as a valuable lesson for all athletes. Like the SEALs, the best teams and athletes in the country emphasize intense practice and train with such a focus on execution through adversity that in competition, it becomes natural. To effectively employ The Switch, it must become automatic, and the only way to make it automatic is to train so that it becomes a natural experience.

11

The Funnel of Focus

Life is hard, and competitive sports are even harder. It challenges the essence of who we are every day and often results in the kind of defeated, low-self-esteem, uncertain person we see so often in this world. But it's not your fault, right? The truth is that the situation itself may not be your fault, but continuing to languish in a lost life without developing a plan to survive is. This is not to say that you're bad, wrong, or a failure; it's just that you haven't yet learned what to do about it.

I reached out to Alan Jaeger, a baseball coach and pitching specialist, to join my MindSide Podcast and share his incredible knowledge about building the arm strength of pitchers. When we started the pre-show discussion, he said that he was happy to talk about arm health and building endurance, but that his passion was the mental game. It wasn't what I had intended, but the lesson I got that day was unmatched.

Jaeger was a high school and college pitcher and coach who worked his way up through the collegiate ranks, only to leave that and start his own pitching program, which focused on mind-body integration. His impact can be seen up and down major league rosters – everything from Cy Young Award winners to the next great draft picks. As we started talking about the mental game, it was clear that his philosophy was very close to mine, but he felt that my approach to the study of focus was much more crystalized than his.

Jaeger told me that every day, and through every experience, we fight against our natural tendency to fall back into the "drama" of the day. Since our default position is often to get caught up in the negativity and chaos of the moment, we tend to quickly abandon our own process, which ultimately makes succeeding, growing and prospering very difficult. This made perfect sense to me. Our ability to focus in competition and throughout life is determined by how we learn to drown out the drama.

Sparking elite focus in competition is a natural experience when life is easy, when we're in the "flow" state, because the external world and its influences have very little impact on our internal processes. If you think about a time when your life or competitive mindset was easy, the intent of your focus was most likely external. For some, that's very easy and very natural, and there are neurophysiological reasons for this. But as Jaeger discussed, the important thing to remember is that it's possible for every person to have a plan and a process helps heighten their focus.

It is important to note that when I'm discussing focus and mental skills as a psychologist, I understand that some clients lack the necessary skills, while others have the skills but have created such mental clutter that they're buried under fears, doubts, indecision, and desire. It all depends on who you are and how you see the world. Some athletes and people simply lack the skills to succeed. They may have the skills necessary for other facets of their lives, but in the area in which they're putting in so much hard work, they may just not have the necessary skillsets.

For example, if I'm working with an athlete on developing a competitive mindset during competition, it's important not to assume that they understand what we consider to be the basics. Breathing is a great example. I like players to have a clear mind when they step into a shot, the gates, or the starting line. Many of these athletes have been so talented for so long that they've been able to overcome some of their inherent limitations, and they may enjoy success in spite of themselves. If I ask them to take a deep breath and clear their mind and they take a deep breath with their shoulders and through their mouth, their belief in how they're performing the simplest of actions can actually have detrimental effects. Everyone knows how to breath, right? Not necessarily, at least not effectively. So it's a skill issue.

On the flip side, there are times when the athlete's mind is so filled with the desire to do things right that they become overwhelmed by too much information. In the heat of the moment, they end up asking themselves what they're supposed to do rather than just doing it – a condition commonly known as "paralysis by analysis." Too many factors are competing for the value and energy of the moment, and this creates a blockage. It's a lot like having too many applications open on your computer – the machine can still execute simple tasks, but if you ask it to take on a more complex operation, it grinds to a stop. The mind is the same way – its capability matches its capacity.

Before delving into the intricate nature of performance focus, it's important to explain, in a performance sense, the distinction between capability and capacity. The **capability** of the mind and performance is what the athlete's underlying ability allows him or her to do. It's the raw material that a trainer or coach has to work with. The **capacity**, on the other hand, is relevant to a particular time and moment – it includes the capability, as well as factors such as the environment and the athlete's health, among others. The capacity to perform also factors in the ability of the athlete to focus on what is important at the moment and filter out other competing factors. This is why evaluating skills and clutter is important. It's never just simple and systematic – it's personal.

In training, you work on two factors: the ability to increase the overall capability and the ability to tap into the maximum capacity when it matters. These are different aspects, and they need to be treated as such. Simplicity is great for some, while others – members of the military, for example – prefer systems and tend to function well in a structured environment. The ability to focus in the heat of the moment is what maximizes the capacity so that it ultimately meets the athlete's capability.

I previously mentioned Jaeger's idea of "drama." I've always conceptualized this as "chaos," and to stay consistent with the three drives described in the earlier chapters, it's important that we treat the terms interchangeably – whether you choose to call it "drama" or "chaos," it's basically the same thing. Remember, the mind is driven to achieve and accomplish goals, to be socially accepted, and to attain stability in life. In the mind and life of every person walking this planet, naturally occurring and man-made distractions, doubts, fears, and clutter rob the mind of the energy it needs to focus. Life and competition is hard, and it takes active engagement and a consistent effort to stay in that frame of mind. That's why the "zone" isn't an ongoing experience, but rather, is episodic.

The chaos of life isn't always chosen. It tends to appear when doubts and fears gain a foothold in the consciousness. From early experiences to recent interactions, a passing thought that was meaningless when the mind was free from stress, fear, or doubt suddenly becomes meaningful and perceived as truth when those factors are present. Insecurities, which are natural for all athletes, become the focus of attention during practice and training, and when they're not redirected, become the focus of outcomes in competition. When mental energy is low or has been damaged, the chaos only increases.

The effort it takes to fight through chaos is exhausting. It's a lot like a poorly maintained dump truck that's carrying a heavy load on low tires and bad shocks – over time, the truck's individual components begin to succumb to the stress and break down. And with each breakdown, other areas of the truck begin to compensate for the broken parts and take on more stress than they were designed for, which only causes further damage. Eventually, a complete overhaul is necessary. This is why the maintenance of individual parts is so important to the overall performance of a machine – or a person.

One of the three needs in life is to maintain order in chaos and find stability. Unfortunately, as Jaeger contended, chaos is actually the norm rather than the exception. During competition, fears, doubts, insecurities, and distractions swarm together to keep the mind defensive and protective. When they become overwhelming, the mind begins to focus internally, becoming more and more concerned with protecting the body's internal movements to create results. This is the trap. Chaos and fear simply love each other, and this has terrible implications.

Heightened pressure environments produce similar results. The increased intensity of a competitive match or one that's played in a large venue raises the collective pressure of the environment, influencing the athlete's thought speed and his or her ability to adhere to their process. It's a lot like a sound system – turning the volume all the way up doesn't improve the quality of the sound, it just overwhelms the listener's senses. But of course, the listener doesn't have to sit there and feel powerless – he or she can simply get up and turn the volume down. In sports, an athlete who's facing adversity, pressure, or fear will often shift their focus inward — away from their targets and intent — and this results in greater challenges and energy expenditure.

The mentally skilled athlete is able to function amidst the chaos, the drama, and the intensity of the moment, and is able to raise their capacity for performance by focusing on their approach. They may not know why, but most describe this ability as a combination of a few factors — trust in their approach, a vulnerability to an outcome, and an ability to re-center themselves prior to heightened activity. What they're describing is what I refer to as "The Funnel of Focus," and it's completely in line with the teachings of other psychologists and mental coaches, much like the model that Alan Jaeger and I share.

The Funnel of Focus [See next page]

Your ability to focus is independent of the clutter, chaos, and drama of your day. There are days when it's aligned and beneficial for performance, and there are other days when it's scattered, counterproductive, and energy-consuming. Let's first consider the athlete who is functioning in a world of chaos and drama, and despite the distractions, is trying hard to perform well.

Regardless of sport, as an athlete approaches the execution phase, there are several steps at work. Athletes who are distracted by the chaos of life and competition fall victim to the Inverse Funnel Effect. Instead of their focus working for them on an external target, it actually works against them by concentrating on internal processes and, most importantly, survival.

Focus is the strongest at the first phase: Awareness. This is the ability of the athlete to examine and experience the moment without judging or labeling. Unfortunately, when an athlete is struggling or in an intense environment, the awareness phase of the funnel is actually where the most energy is directed, because the athlete is in survival mode. The goal becomes simply to survive the challenge, not thrive in it. When survival is the goal, the mind recruits all of its available resources and energy to find safety. This is hardwired into us and is commonly referred to as the "fight or flight" response. The underlying sympathetic nervous system has always had one primary job: survival.

THE FUNNEL OF
focus

NEGATIVE

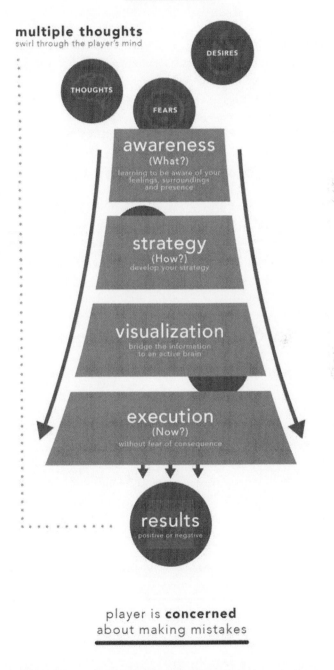

multiple thoughts
swirl through the player's mind

THOUGHTS

DESIRES

FEARS

awareness
(What?)
learning to be aware of your
feelings, surroundings
and presence

strategy
(How?)
develop your strategy

visualization
bridge the information
to an active brain

execution
(Now?)
without fear of consequence

results
positive or negative

player is **concerned**
about making mistakes

But in today's world, although our hardwiring is the same, most of the threats that required such a sensitive and aggressive system when the earliest humans roamed the earth are no longer present. For that reason, the fight-or-flight response system over-interprets and overreacts, although it's still just doing the job for which it was designed.

When an athlete is in a stressful period or struggling with performance, the awareness phase is in full protection mode – it's primarily on guard against ego hits and even greater struggles. As a result, much of the player's focus is taken away from the process or the desired outcome and is spent instead on protection. That changes everything.

When this change occurs, it starts with the Strategy phase. Everything we do in life and in sport has an intent or purpose that, if executed properly, will match the desired outcome. Our strategy is how we intend to execute our game plan. When Awareness is in protection mode, the strategy is no longer about execution for purpose, but rather, for protection. And too many athletes play in this mode far too often.

Regardless of sport, the ability to define a strategy with intent and purpose is important. If a player is functioning in chaos and drama and he or she has reverted to the protective mindset, it'll be hard to change the strategy. It's just difficult for people to commit aggressively to strategy when their mindset is trying to protect them.

When the funnel is inverted, the focus starts to widen as it moves from the narrow point at the Awareness end and outward toward Execution. This wider focus as the execution phase approaches allows the athlete to start searching for solutions and quick fixes and to scan their internal processes. This is why the harder a struggling athlete tries to be more mechanical, the worse things get. It's only when they stop trying to be mechanical that they find their mechanical freedom.

An inverted funnel results in desperate searching, the loss of confidence, an overly internal focus, and often more chaos. You can see it in the face of the athlete caught in the throes of an inversed funnel: they're exasperated, frustrated, and, sometimes, just look like they no longer care. But the opposite is usually the case – they care a lot, but at that moment they care a lot more about protecting themselves from the pain.

When an athlete is playing through the Funnel of Focus, focus flows from wide to narrow – from Awareness through Execution –

to provide the desired Results. On each shot, each pitch, each play, their focus is actively reset to a proper funnel, which is a powerful mechanism to use to move through the indecisions and frustrations of a chaotic environment.

Awareness functions best when it accepts experiences without judgment or reaction. It is important to understand that thoughts, emotions, the chaos of life, and external influences are around us in every experience, and that they're relatively harmless until we assign them meaning or value.

Imagine driving down the road and seeing a car accident. You pull up and see a sixteen-year-old teenager standing outside the car. Without any other information, you're likely to have a variety of passing thoughts, perhaps including "I would hate to be their parent right now," or "They're probably lucky they didn't kill someone – you know how teenagers drive." But those thoughts actually mean nothing, and you're not wrong for thinking them.

Thoughts are random words and sentences that flow through your consciousness. I like to think of them as test balloons from that little voice deep inside you, the one that likes to see if this thought or that thought can elicit a response or emotion from you. Under stress, these thoughts tend to center around fear, stress, and the struggle. In a chaotic world, thoughts tend to be influenced by the angst and chaos of the environment.

Awareness is ultimately acceptance – acceptance that you're okay regardless of the chaos, fears, doubts, and struggles that you're facing. In fact, acceptance is probably the engine behind the effective Awareness that keeps the funnel in the proper form. Without acceptance, awareness is more akin to vigilance. The fight-or-flight instinct only kicks in when we're aware that something may be a threat – hence the analogy to vigilance.

The power to accept ultimately means accepting who you are and having confidence that you can work through any situation in which you find yourself – basically, that you're okay, regardless of your circumstances as a person, athlete, or competitor. If it were only that easy!

If you want to freak someone out, put them in front of a mirror. This definitely demands acceptance. Most of us live in a fairy-tale world, with an often distorted image of who and what we've been, who and what we truly are at the present time, and what we'll become. It's an amazing coping mechanism that allows us to continually attempt to create a new, more successful future for ourselves. Not surprisingly, however, it's also often impossible and inaccurate.

The mirror doesn't lie or distort. It shows you exactly what you are at that moment. It's the truth that we all fear and try to suppress. But the only way to make peace with the mirror is to accept, and acceptance is probably the hardest thing that any of us have to do. It requires us to let go of the past and resist the temptation to seduce the future. Acceptance requires honesty and vulnerability. And as painful as it can be, it also fuels success. When we learn to accept who we are, then we can start growing.

To understand awareness and acceptance, you need to grasp that idea that regardless of circumstance and regardless of challenge, the most significant factor in the equation is you. For an athlete to compete at their best and do so with a funnel that is upright and working for them, he or she must accept and be aware that the challenges of the moment aren't determining their effort or outcome. At the top of the funnel, an open and accepting awareness state allows positive and negative thoughts to move through the consciousness without attachment or labels. If a golfer is concerned about hitting a bad shot, the sudden thought that he or she had better not hit any more bad shots can definitely have an impact on the player. But if their acceptance and awareness is working for them, that thought can move on without impact, a sign that they trust the process and engagement of the funnel.

From an upright funnel, awareness moves to a strategy. No longer about prevention of outcomes, a player who accepts the chaos and intensity of the moment is no longer worried about preventing any outcomes, and he or she understands that the strategy they choose should only be about intent and purpose. If you're going to jump out of an airplane, the strategy should be to jump and effectively deploy the parachute, not hope you survive. Since a strategy is best devised from a mindset of purpose, it should be based on your strengths, not an avoidance of your weaknesses.

An effective strategy should balance the odds of success with the level of commitment to that strategy. The decision with the best odds may not be the easiest to commit to during the heat of competition.

Athletes often have the urge to get out of the box and be a bit more aggressive. That's not necessarily a bad strategy, as long as the decision and outcome, whatever they are, can be fully accepted. Arm-chair quarterbacking is never productive. The biggest question about a using a particular strategy shouldn't be how successful it might be, but rather, how committed you are to the decision to use it.

When the funnel is at risk of turning to the inverse position, the strategy and commitment to it can eroded by doubt, which once again feeds the chaos around you. Commitment requires that you buy in to the plan and ultimately trust it. Once again, it requires acceptance. When an athlete is starting to feed into the chaos and doubts, that acceptance gives away to fear, arm-chair quarterbacking, and a dramatic shift in focus.

Focus isn't about ignoring anything, it's about becoming so locked in on one thing that nothing else matters. Commitment is when the focus is external on the target and the acceptance of the outcome is high. That's when focus becomes intense.

Once the strategy is determined, and the funnel is upright, it's easy to visualize the action. Visualization is the bridge from planning to execution. Visualization is the ability to see the action before the action occurs, not by magic or foretelling, but by creating the desired movie script. There are times when focus is heightened and visualization is easy, but that's not usually the case. In fact, visualization is a skill that should be developed long before it's ever tested in a competitive environment. The ability to focus on the abstract idea of a shot, a pitch, a game, or a race isn't an inherently easy thing to do, primarily because the mind wants to clutter the solitude necessary to visualize effectively.

When the mind sees the intended action with the focused intent, it serves as a rehearsal of positive intent. True visualization should be broken down into two categories: practiced meditation visualization, and active engagement activity visualization.

Practiced meditation visualization is done away from competition while working on relaxation strategies and the meditative mindset. Essentially, you're trying to build the practice to enhance the skill when called upon in competition.

Active engagement activity visualization is visualization that takes place at the moment of action and is so important to a proper funnel of focus. This type of visualization is simply seeing the action you intend to take in a positive, engaged, and active manner. It can be anything that's visualized about the desired outcome: for example, something concrete, like the ball actually going through the net; or something more abstract, like the desired trajectory of your shot passing through an imaginary window that represents the trajectory of a shot. In either case, you should be visualizing the final result or feeling, never the mechanics that produce the result, because that would be visualizing internal actions, and that's when the funnel wants to flip again.

After the visualization bridge, the final aspect of the funnel is the execution. It is simply about attacking the intended action with no reservations or apprehension. Execution is a black-or-white action, one of the few in the sports psychology construct. You're either all in or you're not – there are no in-betweens. Execution comes with a lot of freedom – the awareness is accepting, the focus is on a strategy, and the action has been supported by visualization.

Too many athletes fail to prepare and practice their ability to focus. When the mind happens to align with a heightened focus, it becomes easy, but depending on things to always work themselves out in that way isn't a wise idea. Chaos, drama, doubts, fear, insecurities, expectations, and pressure simply do not work themselves out day after day, week after week. It takes practice to learn how to focus through the thunderstorms that never stop clouding our minds.

12

Breaking Your FishBowl

On October 14, 2012, the Internet slowed to a crawl. Not because of Kim Kardashian or her exploits, but because a man was about to free fall from the edge of space back to Earth.

Felix Baumgartner, an Austrian pilot and world record holder in BASE jumping and wing-suit flying, stood on the step outside his capsule, looked down at the Earth below and saluted. As Baumgartner stood on the ledge of his spacecraft, ready to start his free fall, he said, "Sometimes you have to go up really high to understand how small you are." Without hesitation, he jumped and his record-breaking free fall had begun.

As part of the Red Bull Stratos mission, Baumgartner's jump was the culmination of more than seven years of planning, development, and training. His balloon-tethered capsule left the Earth and rose to an altitude of nearly 128,000 feet, touching the outer layers of the atmosphere and allowing Baumgartner to free fall from a greater height than any human before him. According to the "Red Bull Scientific Summit Summary Report"[7], Baumgartner became the first person to break the speed of sound in a free fall, exceeding 843 mph exactly sixty-five years to the day after U.S. Air Force (USAF) test pilot Chuck Yeager broke the speed of sound in an airplane.

Facing challenging atmospheric conditions that put him into a feared "death spin" – a situation in which the lack of atmospheric resistance results in an uncontrollable and often fatal spinning descent – Baumgartner and his team ultimately overcame the challenges thanks to an intense amount of preparation. He had worked for months with his performance psychologist Dr. Michael Gervais on his performance mindset, and had clarified the roles of each member of his team to limit the clutter, confusion, and uncertainty surrounding such a remarkable jump. Only one person was allowed to speak with him on the radio: Joe Kittinger.

Baumgartner and the Red Bull Stratos mission team had successfully demonstrated the capabilities of human space flight, extending the work started in the 1950s by the USAF and the emerging space program. Joe Kittinger was a USAF test pilot who had answered a request for pilots interested in enrolling in the emerging space development and travel program. Over time, the program shifted its focus to the study of high-altitude pilot ejections, and over the next few years, Kittinger and his team's efforts significantly changed the aviation and space industry.

As documented in his autobiography *Come Up and Get Me*[8], Kittinger successfully executed three high-altitude jumps as part of a program called Excelsior. With each jump, the scientific and engineering teams made significant changes that would prove critical to future success, including Baumgartner's jump. Much like Baumgartner, Kittinger rode a two-thousandths-of-an-inch thick polyethylene balloon to the edges of the Earth's atmosphere, secured in open gondola rather than a space capsule. Scientists at the time were unsure of the danger that falling from such an altitude might pose to the human body, and an earlier jump from 76,000 feet had demonstrated the need to somehow stabilize the free-falling Kittinger. This resulted in the development of a small drogue parachute that would deploy immediately after the jump and create enough atmospheric drag to prevent a deadly spin. In his first high-altitude jump with the drogue, Kittinger lost consciousness when the new chute opened too early, but his emergency chute deployed in time to slow the fall and allow him to land safely.

In a second jump, this one from 74,700 feet, the drogue chute successfully prevented Kittinger from going into an out-of-control spin, and the team was ready for an even higher test. Pushing the limits of the Earth's atmosphere was important because the Air Force had begun to close in on the 80,000-foot altitude mark, and it was critical to determine if pilots could successfully eject from their aircraft under those atmospheric conditions.

The challenge was pushing beyond 90,000 feet. At that altitude, the constitution of the atmosphere is inconsistent with human survival, and a human body will freeze almost immediately if exposed.

On August 16, 1960, Kittinger and the Excelsior team successfully demonstrated survival at high altitudes. In a space suit that was rudimentary by today's standards, his balloon reached an altitude of 102,800 feet. At 50,000 feet, Kittinger noticed that the left glove on his pressurized suit had failed to activate properly; his left hand began to swell to almost twice its size, but he continued to push through the pain and discomfort to complete the mission. Ninety minutes after launch, the balloon reached its high point and Kittinger jumped, free falling for roughly five minutes and reaching a speed of nearly 615 mph. The drogue chute did its job – Kittinger successfully avoided the dreaded death spin and returned safely to Earth. Deemed an American hero, he graced the cover of *LIFE* magazine on August 29, 1960.

The work of the Excelsior team was considered to be a critically important building block of the U.S. space program. It also saved lives. Not long after Kittinger's high-altitude jump, an Air Force pilot was forced to eject from his disintegrating SR-71 reconnaissance aircraft from a height of nearly 83,000 feet. Equipped with his own stabilization drogue chute and flight suit, he managed to survive the ejection and subsequent free fall.

Because of Kittinger's own experience with high-altitude jumps, Baumgartner requested that Kittinger serve as his only contact on the Stratos mission flight radio. Indeed, it was the older aviator's awareness of the emotions and procedures involved in a successful free fall that helped guide Baumgartner back to Earth. When Baumgarter finally descended to 5,000 feet and successfully deployed his parachute, the live feed showed the team celebrating. Two members, however, were a little more subdued: Kittinger and Baumgartner.

As one of the millions who followed the jump online, I was fascinated by the communication between the two adventurers at that moment. Baumgartner, securely attached to his parachute, was communicating directly with Kittinger, requesting wind reports to assist in his navigation to the ground. Only a man who had once pushed the same limits would understand the importance of finishing the task with the same level of focus and execution that was present when Baumgartner stood at the capsule door, ready to jump. It wasn't enough to jump; the less dramatic landing was just as important.

Baumgartner's jump was an incredible feat of engineering, technology, and performance psychology, but Kittinger's effort fifty-two years earlier was another thing altogether. At that time, the only information available on the perils of high-altitude jumping had been gleaned from tests on experimental animals and dummies. Communication was difficult and real-time data monitoring was essentially nonexistent. These factors made the risk to Kittinger's life and limb exponentially greater than what Baumgartner faced a half-century later.

Despite the inherent and often life-threatening challenges, the development of aviation and space technology would continue unabated, and that development required the services of men and women who were willing to challenge the comforts of the known world. Kittinger and the entire Project Excelsior team pushed those boundaries and shattered the existing knowledge base with their jumps, and the aviation and space industry are still benefiting from their innovations today. Breaking the boundaries required the vision and effort of those willing to take the necessary action, without any guarantees of survival or success.

People constantly protect themselves against their own growth. Most of that is fear ("What if I fail when I extend myself beyond my comfort zone?"), and most people are willing to trade the chance for personal development for an assurance that they won't have to face those fears. The internet is full of motivational quotes that address this quandary, everything from "Success happens at the moment the uncomfortable begins" to "You have to fail to succeed." The messages and encouragement are great, but they don't necessarily reduce the shrieking fear that comes with moving outside your comfort zone. Nevertheless, they're fundamentally correct: Growth only happens when the comfort of what is known is abandoned and the risk of what might be possible is embraced. It's the only true formula.

Every day, we're defined by our own limitations. And those structural and perceived barriers don't just come from within – they can also arise from doubts and insecurities of others. Fear is more powerful than gratitude and support because fear has an amazing way of forcing us to retreat in tiny, imperceptible steps. Before we know it, the comfort zones that define our lives have boxed us in.

What we believe is shaped by what we know, what we fear, and how we perceive life to be on the other side of fear. For centuries, common wisdom held that the Earth was the center of the universe. It didn't matter what evidence was presented in opposition; the rhetoric and doctrine of the day said that the sun rotated around the Earth, and anyone who said otherwise was ignored, censored, or punished. The powers-that-be were interested in one thing, and one thing only: uniformity of thought.

When science finally demonstrated with certainty the modern laws of the universe, many people were still not swayed by the overwhelming evidence. What limited their ability to adopt new information? Simple: the fear of abandoning old ideas in favor of new ones. The fear of giving up what we know, even if it's wrong, is more powerful than having to accept new evidence, even when it's based on facts, science, and experience. Fear is all-powerful.

Early explorers – who were afraid to sail to the horizon and the unknown that lay beyond – believed that the Earth was flat. While that may seem illogical and even ridiculous today, the fear of that uncertainty helped shape exploration decisions for generations and limit worldwide growth. It wasn't until explorers were able to push aside their fears and embrace their curiosity and desire for knowledge that they could push those boundaries and emerge with a greater understanding of the world.

The power of boundaries is a mirage. We're a lot like goldfish. Think back to the local county fairs that you may have attended as a child. Every fair that I ever visited had a table full of goldfish bowls and a pile of Ping-Pong balls. If you were able to throw one of the balls into one of the bowls, you won that bowl and the goldfish inside. What a prize! Responsibility! Just what every mom wants – something else to take care of.

So for the entire three or four days of the fair, the goldfish bowls sat there without lids or any other barriers. And yet, the goldfish never tried to escape by jumping out of the bowls. When you took the lucky goldfish home, you may have bought a five-gallon fish tank, filled it with fresh water, lined the bottom with rocks, and put a small plant inside. But never a lid.

That goldfish never outgrew the five-gallon tank. In fact, it never tried to jump out of the bowl, never hit the glass boundary that surrounded it, and never gave up. It just swam in circles all day long, waiting for you to feed it. What a life!

Now, if you maintained your interest long enough to buy a bigger, say, 30-gallon tank and decorate it with a bubbling scuba diver, the goldfish might grow a bit larger. But nothing much would change – it would still just swim around the tank and never try to escape. More importantly, you would never have to purchase a larger tank to accommodate the growth of the fish – it would always grow to match the size of the tank, and no more. Defined by its environment, defined by a thin piece of glass.

We aren't that much different. Our goals, thoughts, and desires are usually defined by the boundaries of our lives. Our minds only grow to the size of our most defining fear. "Pushing the limit" is a great slogan, but it's actually pretty rare among human beings. Most of us become comfortable with the predictable – and avoid the chaos of life and the extension of our boundaries – quite easily.

In a life of boundaries and limitations, extensions, opportunities, and experiences become burdens. Everything is a challenge – nothing is appreciated. Each experience highlights the capabilities that are missed and the additional feelings and work that must be experienced to be functional. The burden mindset is dangerous and destructive. The burdens that build up on your shoulders change life from a search for growth opportunities to one of survival and avoidance. The extra weight is like walking in quicksand, with every step a reminder of the pain you carry.

Burdens are fears. That's not to say that the struggles you face in your game or in your life aren't real, but when we feel the burdens mounting up, our natural tendency is to avoid the pain of the moment. Escape, however, is never really beneficial, because the burdens never really go away. Walking onto the field, the practice range, or the court burdened by the mounting responsibilities that come with our limited boundaries isn't usually a formula for success. It's a mindset of default, not one of determination. It's important to see those same experiences as blessings, opportunities, and challenges. Only then do boundaries become transparent and passable.

Unfortunately, we are too often defined and motivated by fear, which wields power over the strongest humans. Indeed, the desire to avoid painful experiences can limit the outcomes, growth, and progression of entire societies. Athletes, obviously, aren't immune from this – these boundaries define almost all of our lives.

For the mind to grow, boundaries must be shattered, not just extended. The natural tendency in life is to live just inside the limits of our comfort zone. And over time, that boundary shrinks. Our comfort zone gets smaller and smaller every day, until we find ourselves restricted to our daily activities and powerless to take advantage of the potential all around us. Through fear, we restrict, retract, and retreat.

To be successful in life and sport, you must be willing to break your own fishbowl and abandon the limiting fears that have become too comfortable. It is not your failures that define your fishbowl, it's your fears. Fortunately, those fears are usually inaccurate and often simply an illusion. It's not easy to free yourself from them, but it's necessary – and possible.

You won't flounder in obscurity once your fishbowl is broken. You'll be amazed at how well you can function when you have to. Your strengths will continue to be strengths, but once you're outside your comfort zone, you'll learn to trust them more than you ever have.

Learn to trust what you know – certainty is more powerful and useful than hope. Hope may sound like a positive thing, but it actually implies that you have limited control over your actions, not much of an idea of how to succeed, and no idea why you're struggling. When we rely on hope, we abandon process. But when we break the fishbowl, we can let go of hope and trust our own inherent abilities to help us succeed.

Try to allow yourself to experience those feelings of uncertainty without the need to immediately run and hide. Chances are good that you won't get hurt, but if you rush to escape, you'll end up putting more energy into reaching the safety of your boundaries than you would in simply taking part in the experience. It's not the amount of pain suffered but the perseverance used to push through that makes it all worth it.

When you're outside your fishbowl, things will feel completely foreign. That's when you need to work the hardest to appreciate and welcome the challenges of new information, new experiences, and new feelings, without feeling the need to collapse back into survival mode.

Let me give you a golf example.

It is not uncommon for young professional golfers to work their way onto the PGA Tour with passion and a drive to succeed. They're forced to step over and through their competitors at almost every juncture as they fight for the minimal opportunities to secure their future playing rights. Their early mentality is to make it, to get into the conversation, and to have more and more opportunities to play against the world's best. But remember, the mind simply never stops with one achievement. Once they find out that they can actually compete with the world's best, their goal becomes to win. But that takes learning.

As they get used to playing four-day tournaments, they may find themselves every now and then starting the final round one or two shots back of the lead and playing late in the day on Sunday. Now the environment is different – the crowds are larger, and the tension of a final-round, late-afternoon tee time is noticeable even to the most seasoned tour professionals. For a rookie, the pressure can be debilitating, and it's common for them to struggle and quickly fall out of contention when they find themselves in that position. By the end of the round, the emotions that started out as excitement and anticipation rapidly shift to ego-preservation, anger, and frustration. What's worse, many of these young players fail to learn from that experience and environment.

To push boundaries and break fishbowls, you must learn to succeed in these pressure-filled environments. No one has the skillset on speed-dial – you have to know which buttons to push, and that knowledge only comes by first learning the hard way where they are. Final rounds, fourth quarters, and last at-bats all require a player to break through the boundaries and vulnerabilities that are so often exposed in this situations. It's never easy, but those who truly want to learn will see those painful defeats as opportunities.

13

Responsibility Versus
Transferal of Blame

"Coach is not playing me!"

"Coach is playing only the older players!"

"Coach does not like me!"

These are common sentiments that I hear from college and high school athletes. Even worse, I also hear, "Coach is not playing my child, and I think I know why – he's friends with the parents of the other players." It's pervasive in the sporting world, and even worse, it's become part of the fabric of the country we live in today.

Coaches have a difficult job. They must develop training and developmental plans for each player on their team, prepare game plans for the upcoming competitions, and manage the psychological framework of the team, the players, and the people sitting in the stands. Having to manage the "fair playing time" problem only complicates matters.

Athletes who aren't playing as much as they'd like to usually have plenty of explanations. They're not getting a fair shot. They just don't play well in practice. They're in the coach's "doghouse." They haven't been given a chance to get comfortable on the field. The excuse that's usually not given, however, is that they're just not playing well enough for the coach to trust them.

I work with a number of college athletes who work very hard to earn playing time. They feel that they have all the ability in the world, and that they just need a chance to succeed. If they get that chance, the coach will start them more and trust them more. That may be the case, but it's a disastrous scenario.

Your coach does not want an athlete on the field who needs his or her approval to succeed. Coaches want independent, self-driven athletes who compete for the sake of competing, not for the approval and acceptance they might get from the coach, their teammates, or their opponents. More specifically, coaches aren't interested in players who won't take responsibility for their play, who value the coach's impression of them more than they value their own intent.

The best of the best play for themselves and take full responsibility for their play. If they played great, they played great. If they played poorly, they played poorly – and they'll work harder. If you want a coach to play you, adopt that mindset. Embrace responsibility. It's what separates those who succeed and play from those who sit on the bench, blaming the world for their problems.

When I was in high school, I only played one year of varsity baseball. I wasn't good enough to play as a junior on the varsity team, so I was held back. Not only was I one of the youngest students in my grade, but my maturity clock was behind. I didn't really grow until my senior year, and it took several more years after that for me to fully mature.

My summer league baseball coach was often the target of my blame and frustration. When I was a sophomore, after my first junior varsity season, I played on our summer-league team in Baton Rouge. Our coach that season was a legend around south Louisiana, not just for sports, but also as the legendary lead singer for John Fred and His Playboy Band. While still in college, John Fred Gourrier had written and sung the No. 1 hit, "Judy in Disguise (With Glasses)," a takeoff of the Beatles' "Lucy in the Sky with Diamonds." The song ran up the charts thanks to its great lyrics and dance beat. John Fred (as he was called by all his players and friends – we rarely even uttered his last name) was a college athlete who graduated from my high school and would go on to coach competitive baseball teams when he wasn't touring around playing music festivals. He had a lot of time to coach baseball, and he really enjoyed his time on the diamond.

Our team was very talented, and we practiced around the clock. Batting practice before games often lasted two hours in the deep Louisiana heat, and even though I was a pitcher, I was also required to catch batting practice every day. I wasn't one of the top pitchers on the team, but I thought I should have been. Obviously, my belief was greater than my ability at the time. Every time I saw my name listed as batting-practice catcher, I knew it meant I wasn't going to play that night. My job, apparently, was simply to be a batting-practice catcher.

I used to steam, literally and figuratively, as I caught batting practice. It's a thankless job, and the BP catcher is often the forgotten part of the practice session. As batting practice came to a close, the rest of the team would start gearing up for the game, while I'd wobble into the dugout to rest. I hated that summer, and I despised John Fred for not playing me. In my mind, he had it out for me because I hadn't played on his previous summer teams.

The truth, however, was that I just wasn't good enough. I started three games on the mound that year. In the first game, I threw a four-inning no-hitter against one of the worst teams in the league. My second start was against the top team in the league, but it was also the last regular-season game. I threw a seven-inning complete-game victory, and even though the other team was resting their starters, I thought it was even more evidence that I should be starting more. My last start of the summer came in the semifinals of the area tournament against the same team. This time, I struggled and took the loss. I was angry and frustrated, but not for losing the game. I was upset that I hadn't gotten enough chances during the year. In my mind, if I'd pitched more innings, I wouldn't have struggled in that game. Honestly, I missed the lesson.

After the season, I was still angry and more than willing to shift the blame for my poor outing to coach John Fred. He'd done me wrong, I thought, and hadn't developed me as a pitcher. Little did I know that I was falling into a trap that trips up many, many young athletes.

I wanted more than anything to be accepted by my coach (think back to one of the three drives of the human mind) and to be validated as one of his guys. When I failed to receive that acceptance, I lashed out with blame rather than looking inward and learning through the challenge. It was his fault that my level of play wasn't good enough or consistent enough to give the team a competitive outing in every start. The reality, of course, was that it was just easier to blame him than it was to accept full responsibility for my performances and to work to improve.

As the next season approached, John Fred was again our summer-league coach. This time around, however, I was one of his ace pitchers (and I didn't have to catch batting practice, either). We had a better team and won the city championship. Before the All-Star team was selected and preparations made for the World Series tournament schedule, John Fred pulled me aside in the dugout. It was just the two of us.

He started to talk to me about the previous season and my development not only as a player, but as a man. He told me how he had built his music career and played with some of the world's best, including Elvis Presley and the Beatles. I was mesmerized by the fact that he was telling me stories that no one else on the team knew about. I remember sitting there and thinking that I'd been accepted into his inner circle. He then asked me if I knew why he had worked me so hard at catcher last year? I told him I thought it was because the team needed me in that role. He looked at me and said, "No, *you* needed that role."

I didn't fully understand what he was trying to tell me. I was still harboring some anger and frustration against him, and I felt that while I'd had a good year, some of the scars and bruises hadn't healed. I asked him to explain.

He told me that I hadn't been good enough the year before to do much more than catch batting practice, along with a few spot starts and other small appearances. While the team in fact needed a batting-practice catcher, that role wasn't particularly vital to the team's success. He knew I was angry and that I resented being in that role, but he wanted me to take some responsibility for my own improvement and to use my anger as motivation. It all began to make sense. He was right. I was young, mentally soft, and more than anything, I'd been looking for his validation and approval. Catching batting practice in 95-degree heat for two hours every day was none of that – but in the same breath, it was all of that.

After the all-star team was selected, we won our regional tournament, then our state tournament, and eventually won the World Series. I played a critical role on the mound, and we surpassed the success of any team that John Fred had coached. That team had probably ten of the fifteen players go on to play in elite Division I baseball, and we were just getting started. I was just getting started too. Our conversation was a catalyst, because I started taking responsibility and stopped blaming others.

My first formal meeting with the LSU baseball team in the fall of 1990 drove this point even further. Coach Bertman stood in front of the team in the team lounge and talked about the expectations for the fall season, the ideals and pillars behind his system, and what was expected of the players. The previous year's team had finished third in the country and was returning the nucleus of the production, both on the mound and throughout the lineup.

He started by asking us what we thought the national pastime was. It seemed like a no-brainer for a locker room full of baseball players. The national pastime was obviously baseball, peanuts, hot dogs, and Cracker Jack. It had been that way for more than a century. Easy.

But Coach Bertman shook his head and told us that actually, the "transfer of blame" had become the national pastime, and we weren't going to fall into that trap. When players, teams, and coaches blame others for their circumstances, their failure to accept responsibility simply shows that they lack the willpower necessary to make their success a reality. When a player blames an umpire for a bad call, blames a professor for giving them a C instead of a B, and blames a coach for not playing them, they're giving the power to factors that have no immediate ability to influence the outcome. Those who blame immediately lose their power.

He was right. John Fred was right. I was blaming coaches and circumstances for my failure to consistently succeed in baseball.

The best players in the world may occasionally seem as though they're blaming circumstances, coaches, officials, and weather conditions, but by and large, they've learned the value of taking responsibility for their actions. Unfortunately, the transferal of blame has become an epidemic in today's society. It's such an automatic reaction now that players, coaches, parents, and commentators don't even realize they're falling for it.

Umpires and officials are going to make bad calls. Making calls is their job, and that job is hard. One way to prevent bad calls from impacting your performance is to put yourself in a position that makes those calls irrelevant. A pass interference penalty on fourth down in the fourth quarter may very well change the outcome of the game, but it wouldn't have that power if you'd been focused in the first three quarters and up by 28 points. At that point, the call is merely a nuisance, not a game-changer.

If you're playing for a coach's validation and approval, you're not accepting responsibility for your own influence on your game. We all want approval and acceptance; it's a natural human desire. But when we move our validation needs to an external source, we open the door for more transferal of blame and less acceptance of responsibility.

Accountability and responsibility are the pillars of an elite mindset.

Accountability, in my book, is doing what you're charged with to make yourself better. When you look in the mirror, your accountability should be to yourself. There should be no shortcuts and no self-delusion. The ultimate question should be, "Am I doing everything I can to make myself better?" Remember, you're not accountable to anyone but yourself. Validation becomes an internal fulfillment.

Responsibility is the burden you accept to ensure that your actions respect the efforts of those around you. If you're responsible for packing a colleague's parachute as they prepare to jump out of an airplane, can they trust that you've given 100 percent of your attention to the task? That's a responsibility that can't be taken for granted.

Teams and elite players function in a culture of accountability and responsibility. Each player is presumed to have done whatever's necessary to improve and train themselves, so that under pressure, each player is responsible for giving their all to every other team member, without question. At that point, through the good and the bad, there is no more room for blame. Everyone is giving their best. The outcome ultimately may not go your way, but the effort is always given without question.

Each day that I squatted down to catch batting practice, my responsibility to the team was to be present and to demonstrate commitment to the team's goals. Unfortunately, I wasn't holding myself accountable. My validation needs weren't focused on me, but instead on what my teammates and coach thought of me. Thankfully, the team was good enough to overcome my pity parties. The blame that I directed towards coach didn't derail my ultimate goal, but once I had some insight into his motivations, I felt very guilty about the blame. It was a very hard summer, but I learned some great lessons from it.

If every player took care of his or her business and understood that playing time was never a given, every team would be better. The challenge for a talented team with great players sitting on the bench is for the coaches to clearly define each player's role. Players don't generally become accountable and responsible by themselves. Athletes are inherently competitive and prone to making comparisons with others, but to be successful that must be tempered.

To enhance your own accountability and ultimately your responsibility to the team, consider these points:

- When you get caught up in the actions of others and blame others for your circumstances, you lose your power. Imagine if you could retain that power for your own game – how much more successful would you be?

- If you were playing full-time and were successful every time, would you be learning the same things that you're learning right now?

- If no one took credit and no one was blamed, how would your game be different?

- If you can't trust yourself to be the determining factor behind your own success, who can you trust more? A coach? A teammate? An umpire?

Great teams are built with players who appreciate and understand the concept of responsibility. It's never easy to stand in front of the team or any group of people to take responsibility. But it's even harder to do so in front of a mirror. It's a lot easier to hide behind the failures or the perceived deficiencies of others than it is to accept personal responsibility. The only way to develop an elite competitive mindset and to ensure continued success in whatever you do is to take responsibility for one's actions.

14

Vulnerability and Loss Aversion

When I was growing up, I lived for a time in a small military suburb in southern Illinois, across the Mississippi River from St. Louis. It was great because most of the families living in the community were in the same situation that we were – they were military families with young children who were used to moving every three years. It was normal for families to move in and out of the neighborhood. There was a constant influx of kids.

Our house backed up to another house, and the two backyards came together to serve as a gigantic playground. Because our house was the first house on a cul-de-sac, traffic was light and it was a safe place for the neighborhood children to play. It was a perfect environment for me. The sun determined the schedule, and our dad's whistling from across the neighborhood at dinnertime signaled the two-minute warnings.

As the seasons changed, so did the sports we played. In the fall, there was a pickup football game every day after school. Anywhere from four to fourteen players might show up, but a game was always going on. In the spring, football gave way to baseball, with scrap wood for the bases. Because we didn't have many organized practices for our formal league teams, my backyard became my practice field.

What made that backyard on Farragut Court so unique and fertile was that we didn't have age limits or age matching. If you showed up, you played. I was a good baseball player, but I got better as a fifth-grader trying to hit off of the ninth-grade pitcher. In fact, he struck me out more than I hit him, but I worked hard to find a way to beat him. I used to sit in class and think about how to hit him in the afternoon.

There was nothing worse than being the next batter up and hearing the whistle of one of the dads calling the kids home for dinner. I had to sit with my frustration until the next day.

Today's young athletes don't learn their game in the backyard, on the playground, or in their driveways. Instead, today's athletes train in structured environments such as skills camps, and they have access to intense skill coaching. Large private training centers, while ideal in both theory and practice, have also resulted in widespread acceptance down the ladder of player development that *more* coaching is better. While that may be the case in a laboratory setting, what seems to be sacrificed is the ability of the athlete to "figure it out." Having worked in one of those academies, the hardest thing to stop was the athlete from relying too heavily on the coach for immediate feedback when something didn't go right, AND stopping the coach from immediately stepping in to provide feedback. That type of relationship may take away the self-exploration and self-determination that older generations possessed.

My company, The MindSide, benefits from the new style of coaching because more and more coaches and parents want to gain whatever advantage they can, and the mental game is a common area for improvement. And who can blame them? Who wouldn't want every single advantage that these settings and programs offer? The problem is that we may be overlooking a very important factor: vulnerability. With all the focus on ways to improve, the industry may unknowingly be placing more and more pressure on the athletes to NOT FAIL. The reason is simple – when the comprehensive new training centers, increased number of sports psychologists, improved, science-based coaching techniques, and overall growth in technology contribute to success, it's natural to notice their benefits. But when success is elusive, only the athlete is left to blame. That may not be accurate or fair, but athletes connect those dots all the time. And while all the modern, newfangled ways to train aren't really the problem, they *are* easy targets when performance doesn't improve.

Older generations of athletes learned to play sports on playgrounds, in backyards, or through unstructured programs. Those environments were breeding grounds for vulnerabilities – you had to call your own fouls, balls and strikes, and compete against older, more gifted players. But this allowed you to learn how to use what you had to compete against those who were better.

Vulnerability and Loss Aversion

The greatest challenge facing an emerging athlete is the ability to accept vulnerability. And the only way to become vulnerable is to compete against everyone, including those who are better than you and those who are not, and learn to be able to handle every possible outcome. Today's athlete doesn't necessarily train to compete, they train to survive and "make it." But learning the game is about more than "perfection zones," or how to play and compete only when you're doing it right. Athletes need to learn how to compete under less than ideal circumstances, and with less coaching and less instruction. And that's what vulnerability is – it's about knowing what you have and how to compete with it without constant correction.

We often hear that you "must fail to succeed." That's definitely true, but probably not for the reasons that many think. Failure is never the goal, but the impact of a failure can be a positive step toward a desired outcome if an athlete's mindset is about engaging rather than surviving or escaping. For growth to happen through failure, the player must know that he or she is okay to work through the failure, that it's not the end of the road.

Failure must always be an option in competition. The newer generation of athletes plays to prevent failure, and they often do so through "If-Then" statements. These work something like this:

"If I can get my mechanics to work for me today, then I think I can compete."

"If coach gives me more opportunities, then I think I can show him or her that I'm ready to play, and having his or her confidence will help me."

"If I can't make mistakes early in the game, then I'll allow myself to become more aggressive."

The use of If-Then statements hampers performance because it puts the avoidance of negative outcomes ahead of the desire to achieve. To be successful, you must never use the avoidance of a feared outcome as your motivation. When the mind is cluttered with commands to avoid potentially threatening outcomes, it simply lacks needed mental resources to achieve and succeed in the competitive experience. With the tiny differences between success and failure in sports, any stolen mental energy devoted to protecting against failure is simply robbing the focus from succeeding. The mind only functions when it is locked into its desire and fully accepting of the outcome, either way.

It is a vulnerability issue more than anything. Those who learned to play in the backyard understood the concept, because if they couldn't learn to overcome the failures, then the challenges of the backyard would beat them down. If-Then statements don't sustain excellence – they just limit growth. But why have If-Then statements become so pervasive?

We live in a culture where our youth and emerging athletes are defined by an unrealistic sense of what normal or average athletic talent looks like. I'm often asked what it takes to succeed in college or to transition to professional sports. Before I answer, I ask the person what *they* think it takes to play sports at the college or pro level. I'm almost always amazed to hear what most people believe is the norm, because it's much closer to the extreme.

Let me give you an example. I was working with a young emerging junior golfer who had been recruited heavily by several prominent college programs. They all had her on their watch lists, but several had told her that while they were interested in her and felt that she'd be a great long-term player for their program, they had offers out to other players who were better scorers in competition. The father, smartly, asked what differentiated the other players from his daughter, so that she could work on improving those areas. One coach told him that while his daughter's scoring average of 75 in large invitational tournaments was very good, they were looking for golfers who regularly posted scores in the 72-73 range and could shoot 75 on a tough day.

It's amazing to look at that coach's present roster – she currently doesn't have one player who's shooting those numbers. What changed? Why have her expectations changed?

When you set unrealistic expectations and communicate them to the athletes, you're transforming the perceived ideal into the standard. The result is the mental error of overlooking reality in an effort to see what you believe in their performance, and this goes for both positive and negative experiences.

This college coach may have a completely different reason for not pursuing this junior golfer, but I hear similar explanations way too often, which only help to create false ideals about athletes and their performance. Here are just a few (along with my rebuttal):

- High school pitchers should throw in the low to mid 90s to be a college recruit.
    - Major League pitchers don't throw that hard up and down the pitching roster, so why should a high school pitcher?
- Golfers should compete to win 80 percent of their tournaments.
    - According to statistician Rich Hunt of Pro Golf Synopsis[9], PGA Tour players win 80 percent of their annual income in only 20 percent of their events. In other words, they compete to win in five to ten of the twenty-five they play on average each year.
- If I can get some more playing time, I know I'll succeed. I just need live reps in a game.
    - Playing time is determined by a variety of factors, and if you're not playing as much as you think you should, there are a few ways to remedy that. Becoming better in practice is the first avenue to more playing time. The second one is that when your time finally comes to take the field, don't try and make up for perceived wrongs. Instead, play for that moment only – play only for what the competition demands of you at that point in time.
- If I can get a few good games under my belt, I'll become more comfortable in the game.
    - Confidence is not built through results. It can help, but it's not built there. It's built through the developmental process. The only thing you'll gain by pressing in early-season games is more frustration, unless you refocus on competing after each one.

This process isn't just reserved for the athletic world, either. When my oldest daughter was going through the college-selection process, my wife and I were shocked when college recruiters showed us the "average academic and testing scores" from their last incoming freshman class. There's no way I would have qualified for college as a high school senior under today's standards. The scores for the state college she now attends – a very highly ranked state college, mind you – were off the charts. I was actually concerned that she might not get in, and she's a very bright student! But she did, and she's handled her course load extremely well.

The pressure to simply "make it" has risen to such extraordinary levels that many young people are simply not prepared to handle it. We all know that the world is competitive and that it's important to prepare our children for that competition, but the relentless pressure and resulting workarounds that we see today are causing more problems, not fixing them. We've stopped teaching young athletes and students to actually learn and have instead reduced ourselves to just giving them tips on how to clear the hurdles. The goal has shifted.

"Making it" and finding our way through life can be accomplished in an infinite number of ways, and there are no signs or courses that can teach you how to battle through your vulnerability to succeed. It's all about facing life challenges on our own and not protecting anyone else from their own challenges. Our life experiences are a perfect training ground.

When I was a senior in college, I received a phone call from a fan of the baseball program who asked if I knew anyone who was looking for a job over the holidays, from Thanksgiving to the first week of January. The job was to work with a civil engineering crew supporting local construction and development. The pay was really good – $10 an hour – and the job was sunup to sundown. I called my dad and asked him if he thought we knew anyone who might be interested. He said, "Yeah – you."

I had just changed my major to psychology. It was an unorthodox time to do that, but I felt it was something I needed to do if I wanted to start following my new life passion. Nevertheless, I decided to apply for the job, and I was hired. I started working for the crew after finals in late November and completed all of the necessary OSHA, worksite-safety, and other construction-crew certifications. I had no idea what I was doing – I just knew that I had to show up ten minutes before the sun rose and could leave ten minutes after it set. If it rained, I still had to show up, but I might not work or get paid – only days on which work was actually performed counted toward my paycheck, and rainouts were just part of the job.

One of my first tasks in early December was to wade through "Devil's Swamp," a backwater north of Baton Rouge that lay between the Mississippi River and a chemical plant that specialized in cleaning contaminated water and returning it to the water supply. Devil's Swamp was allegedly one of the most toxic bodies of water in the United States — as the older workers in my crew explained, untreated waste had simply been dumped into the water there in the early days of the refinery industry. My job was to wade around in chest-deep water, chart the pipes that had been installed years before, and update the maps. Even though it was December, it was still an ominous sign when I realized that I was standing in a body of water in south Louisiana that was completely devoid of wildlife. I guess you could say I'm lucky to have healthy children after that adventure.

Later that month, I worked on a construction crew on the Mississippi River, counting, charting, and evaluating the number of times the "hammer" pounded the large industrial support beams. There is nothing like riding on a John boat on the Mississippi River, before dawn, with eight other construction workers, a small engine propelling us through the heavy currents of such a huge, majestic waterway. At lunch, the guys all gave me the same advice: "Finish college, learn from your mistakes, and never quit fighting for your dream."

The work was tough. I normally came home at night and went right to bed. I had a 45-minute drive to the river, so I usually left the house around five in the morning and got home at six that evening — if I didn't have baseball practice. On those nights, I wouldn't get home until 7:30 or so, at which point I'd just eat and go to sleep. I had just gotten engaged to my girlfriend (now wife), and we had no nightlife, no time to plan the wedding, nothing. I was exhausted.

I worked right up until the day we reported back for baseball in early January. Just before training started, I had lunch with my dad. He was the older of two boys from a suburban Cleveland family. His father was a first-generation immigrant, and his mother was the daughter of German immigrant farmers. Neither had stayed in school beyond the fifth grade. Nevertheless, my grandfather, who was a carpenter, had a brilliant mathematical mind. My dad told me that during his high school and college summer vacations, he worked as a carpenter's apprentice for his dad. Cleveland winters are notoriously freezing, grey, and snowy, but the summers are also stiflingly hot and humid. He said that carrying shingles up and down wooden ladders to his father and his father's crew on those brutal summer days reminded him of the power of an education. He also told me that he had arranged my winter construction job for me so that I could learn the value of hard work. The goal, he explained, wasn't to make $10 an hour, but to earn self-respect by fighting through the challenge of hard work. Lesson learned. After that holiday job, my college GPA rose sharply – I went from a 2.8 average to nothing lower than a 3.8 in my final undergraduate semester and then my entire graduate school career.

It would have been easy for my dad to enroll me in a full-time training program, but an important lesson would have been lost. He didn't want to make things easy – he wanted to reinforce the importance of a work ethic to a successful life.

Are we doing our athletes a disservice by making these training centers and tutoring sessions available to them? I would say absolutely, unequivocally no – but we do need to prepare them better.

Perfection is never the goal. We don't have the ability to Photoshop our pictures of life and performance and produce the image we want. Scores are scores – outcomes are outcomes. They can't determine value. As parents, coaches, and athletes, the good and the bad must remain simply scores that contribute to our overall development.

It's easy to protect against the pain of disappointment. If a young athlete has a bad game, it's easy to quickly pack up and leave, call the specialist coach and schedule a private lesson. At that moment, everyone has been seduced into the black hole created by a lack of vulnerability. By immediately leaving the game, you're losing a perfect opportunity to "lose like a winner" by sticking around and congratulating the victors. Learn to show the others that win or lose, your demeanor, as a coach, parent, or athlete doesn't change. Stick around and be strong about it without making excuses.

By calling a specialist coach to fix the problem, the mentality shifts away from working through things to fixing problems. The If-Then statement returns: "If I can fix this mistake, then I can play well." To truly play with vulnerability on your side, it's important to put things in perspective, to tell yourself, "I may not be doing this particularly well right now, but I'll compete through it." Avoid the temptation to take the easy way out.

This doesn't mean that you don't work on your flaws. On the contrary, by embracing vulnerability and accepting that you're okay to work through the program, the lessons that you've had in the past will actually work. In other words, if you do what you've trained to do and get back to those fundamentals, you won't need an emergency session. The problem is that negative feelings and frustration trump the development of validation, especially when a detour that avoids all the problems is theoretically available.

Being truly vulnerable requires understanding the influence of validation sources. Often referred to as intrinsic or extrinsic motivators, I see these as outside factors that validate your performance. Are you competing, training, and working for yourself, or are you doing it for someone else, or something else, or even just for what it means?

The best of the best do it for themselves. That may sound selfish, and it is – in a good sense of the word. When we give those around us the power to influence how we feel, we're searching for external validation to let us know that we're capable. The problem is that such external validation is never enough. All we do is raise the bar after every success. That increases our aversion to vulnerability, because deep down our own acceptance of who we are isn't good enough – we need someone else to give us that approval.

People who are internally validated compete and train for what it means to them. There's often an internal hunger, a chip on the shoulder that drives them. That chip is what they use to stand on – to get up in the morning, to go to the gym, and to get through competition. It's their driving motivation, and it comes from within. Yes, a coach's encouragement or criticism will have an impact on them, but more from a confirmation than a validation standpoint. They appreciate their vulnerabilities and work through them. For those who are truly internally validated, their vulnerabilities become fuel for their success.

When we can let go, and understand that we're capable of working through the difficulties, success can begin.

Far too often, however, the threat of losing outweighs the benefits of winning. It's not just about losing games, but losing pride, respect, playing time, and emotional confidence, among other psychological factors that we often cling to so strongly. The power of the human mind to prevent losing out of fear of the adverse psychological impact is impressive. It's not a high-level psychological process but a primal survival response. Losing at something can almost become the equivalent of a matter of life or death.

The difficulty of allowing oneself to be fully vulnerable in the face of a win or a loss may not be a flaw in our thinking, but one rooted in our general psychological disposition. One of the leaders in the field is Dr. Daniel Kahneman. Kahneman was awarded the Nobel Prize in Economic Sciences in 2002 (along with Vernon L. Smith) for his work in understanding the psychology of judgment and decision-making in everyday choices and the financial markets.

In his book, *Thinking Fast and Slow*[10], Kahneman explored the decision-making process of individuals throughout the course of the day, examining the simple and complex decision matrices that commonly influence decisions in law, business, investing, and sport. The categorical nature of decision-making involves a complex matrix of choices influenced by both an emotional drive and a rational perspective. The emotional tends to be more of an instinctual perspective, while the rational involves a more systematic analysis of risk and benefits. Effective decision and risk-taking behaviors require a delicate balance and a deeper understanding of both the nature of such decisions and the drives behind them in each individual. As decisions become more "important," the interaction between the two cognitive "systems" of the mind influences the final decision and post-action evaluation. Kahneman adopted terminology from earlier psychologists Keith Stanovich and Richard West, and clarified that System 1 is the more automatic and "intuitive" decision making process, while System 2 relates to more effortful, purposeful decision making. It is this balance between the two systems that highlights the complex cognitive decision-making in competitive environments, not just every day life.

As I read his work on decision-making and its possible influence on sport, it became evident that one of the strongest guiding factors for athletes is a concept called *"loss aversion."*

Imagine that I told you I was going to give you $50,000, but to access the money you had to bet half of it – $25,000 – on one hand of blackjack. The deal is that if you win the hand you get to keep the $50,000 plus any winnings from the bet, and if you lose, you can take the remaining $25,000 and walk away. No taxes, no reporting (unfortunately, this isn't real life, so you'll have to suspend your disbelief for the sake of this example). All yours.

Easy question and scenario – of course you'll take the bet. What do you have to lose, right?

Now, as the cards are being dealt out, you receive a face card (a 10-point King, Queen, or Jack), and a three of clubs. You're sitting on 13. As the dealer, I immediately turn over my cards and show you that I have a blackjack. You lose.

You were beaten without ever having a chance to win. As a result, you lose the $25,000 bet.

Are you going to keep playing?

Walk away?

Change the bet?

This is an interesting question that parallels so much that happens in life and sport. When I give this scenario in large groups, about 80 percent of the audience says they'll take the $25,000 and walk away. Most of these people say something like, "This is a lot of money, I don't want to lose any more, and it's better to leave with something than nothing." The consistency with which some variation of this answer is given is amazing.

Of the remaining 20 percent who'd stay and continue to play, roughly half say that they'd put some of the money in their pocket and play with the rest. While they see themselves as taking more of a risk than those who want to walk away with the full $25,000, these "partial savers" are falling into the same trap of mitigating losses. It doesn't matter if they think they're being aggressive – they've created a safety net that guarantees some victory.

In the back of the room, there is always the one person who gets the audience thinking. In one of the groups where I gave this scenario, the head coach of a highly ranked team stood up and said, "I'm in it to win as much as I can." When I asked the coach, in front of his team, why he was willing to risk everything when the odds were obviously stacked against him (especially after losing the first hand), the coach started to explain. But before he could provide me with his rationale, one of the other players yelled, "Hey, coach, you make a lot more than us, and we don't have the money you have!"

The coach laughed, but before he could give me his explanation, I asked the entire team, including the 80 percent who chose to take the guaranteed $25,000 and walk away, who else would be willing to stay and play. As it turns out, he wasn't the only one who wanted to stay and play, but he had the highest profile of anyone in that organization, so it was a perfect learning example. About five other players and coaches stood up with coach – roughly five out of a hundred.

Coach said, "I would stay and play because even though I just lost, I didn't earn the money. It was given to me. I have a chance to win more than I started with today. If I lose it, it will sting, but I want to win more than I want to prevent losing any more money. How many chances do I get where I have nothing to lose? For me, it's about winning. I can always make more money, but the chance to win is so powerful to me. It's what drives me."

Coach was exactly right. According to Dr. Kahneman, there is a constant psychological battle being waged where there is a decision that is influenced by potential value to the person, such as financial decisions or outcomes of sporting events. With every scenario, the psychological impact of a loss outweighs the perceived psychological benefit of winning or gaining for the average person. At a core level, we're all driven harder to avoid losses than to achieve success. Even though you could gain more than you could lose, the fear of losing what you have or a future amount is significantly stronger than what you could gain or win. Kanheman refers to as the Loss Aversion Ratio[11], and the coefficient that guides decision making in the face of a loss needs to be greater than 2x the gain over the impact of a loss. When the impact of the loss involves psychological processes such as pride, value, validation, playing time, and factors common in sport, the perceived gain must be significantly greater than the psychological loss.

This is particularly evident when players set smaller goals or thresholds of success, such as playing just well enough to not lose a game. Once the smaller goal is achieved, the mind doesn't free up; instead, it becomes satisfied and stops. This is why If-Then statements simply don't work when it comes to performance. The feared outcome is avoided, but the desire isn't achieved.

Once small losses are experienced, the mind goes into overdrive to prevent future losses. That's the critical point of the blackjack example. The key is that the first hand was lost. Even worse, the hand was lost without any opportunity for you to compete. The odds were proverbially stacked against you. Before the loss, it's all fun and games. Once the loss is incurred, however, the mind starts to evaluate risk, value, and what can be achieved in the face of the loss. The small goals, or If-Then statements, start to work overtime.

"If I can just leave with $25,000, I won't feel as bad about losing $25,000."

"If I can get my original $50,000 back, then I will walk away."

"If I have to tell my family that I had $25,000 in my hands and lost it all, then they'll think I was being reckless. My family could really use that money."

Coach had it right, however. The truth is that the money was given to you. Even if you earned it, you could always earn more. Yes, it would be painful, but not devastating. You can always recover. But the mind takes over, especially after a loss, and starts to evaluating what the potential impact of future losses would be. It seems easier to say that the money and potential losses would be less if given to you, but once you hold the money, it all changes. The fact is this – as pressure mounts, the potential for loss aversion increases.

Now, I'd prefer that in real life, you bet on you – with a solid strategy and effective preparation for the challenge – and stack the percentages in your favor for competition. But this example highlights the overpowering drive behind loss aversion.

Basketball shooters often overvalue the number of shots missed rather than the number made.

Baseball hitters remember the times they were struck out, not the number of hits they had.

Golfers who are putting for birdie may hope to make the birdie putt, but deep down, the driving force is to avoid the three-putt and ruin par.

In fact, in *Thinking Fast and Slow*, Kanheman highlights a study that was authored by economists Devin Pope and Maurice Schweitzer.[12] In this study, the authors demonstrated that golfers at the highest level, on the PGA Tour, had significantly greater success putting for par than birdie, controlling for all the factors that may influence outcomes. By "trying harder" on pars, players were trying to avoid bogeys more than making birdies, which is seen as a missed opportunity to gain an advantage. In fact, it is my experience, that the potential gain of a birdie is often overshadowed by the worrisome fear of having a chance of a birdie but three-putting for a bogey. A double whammy.

How many games, rounds, practice sessions, and tournaments have been all about preventing future losses? More than we can probably imagine, although the motivation behind it is natural. That can be overridden, though.

The five who stood up with their coach were also different than the rest of the team. They were the team leaders in a number of areas, both on the field and in the locker room. Over the course of the season, those who stood up wound up having the best years. It was unreal to see how it played out in real life.

The challenge to the team was to see everything as an opportunity to increase vulnerability and focus on achieving rather than preventing. Simply put, loss aversion can be overridden, and in order to be successful, *must* be overridden. The underlying patterns that the human mind wants to trust and use to enhance comfort aren't always correct for you in the heat of competition.

Too many players and coaches get caught up in trying to validate practice, confirm past performances, and maintain success. When struggles occur, the prevention of future struggle sends the brain into a default position of more prevention. If-Then statements take over. You have to be willing to walk away with zero and trust that in the future, you'll have, create, or fight for more opportunities. Furthermore, you have to accept that if you lose, it doesn't define you any more than you allow yourself to be defined by it. You're capable of losing and surviving. You're vulnerable to the outcome because you're capable of persevering and working through it.

The work that you've invested in your game – all the practice and gym work – isn't invalidated by good or bad performances. It's been invested and is waiting to mature. The reason you train is not to prevent failure, but to succeed. Being vulnerable to the outcome allows you to push for the big winnings, not simply cover the minimal costs.

The best of the best are willing to risk the "What If" for the next scenario and challenge. Too many other people, however, are busy thinking ahead to their next move, but from a protective position. It's as though they're already thinking about limiting any damage. Much too often, the fear of the "What If" is greater than the desire to achieve.

To be successful, you must not only be willing to be vulnerable and open to the ultimate outcome, but understand that in competition, the smaller battles don't define the outcome. Yes, there are critical points in all competitions, but facing them with apprehension is never a formula for success. It's important that every player, competitor, and athlete approach the circumstances at hand with intention of purpose, not prevention.

15

What If?

When I was a kid I used to suffer from a pretty good case of anticipatory anxiety. On the way to school or on the way to the ballpark, I normally found myself becoming more and more nervous. Unfortunately, this never really went away – it's kind of who I am today, but I think I've learned how to deal with it, at least consistently better than when I was a kid.

I often found myself worrying about the future, or whether a coach or teacher was upset with me, or what the implications would be if I messed up. It was a pretty painful feeling to know that you were doing everything you could to put yourself in a good position but were still worried about disappointing your coaches and teachers.

It's more unfortunate when you understand that everything in my life growing up was really, really good. I remember sitting down with my mom and telling her about my anxiety, and she would always say, "When you feel it, don't fight it, just question it." She would also say, "What's the worst that could happen?" It seems like a simple question, but the answer doesn't come very easily to people who constantly worry about what the future may hold. For these people, the worst that could happen is at best an abstract concept.

It's something about the future that you just can't put your finger on. When left to its own devices – particularly in folks who worry about the future – the mind can make some downright scary connections. It's no different in sports. What is this season going to hold? How am I going to do? How is coach going to respond to my play? These are all things that sometimes derail an athlete's ability to perform. But then again, what's the worst that could happen?

The mind works in extremes and it struggles with gray areas. It prefers to see things as black or white, all or nothing. When new information is taken in and processed, the mind tries to categorize and simplify these memories and experiences to increase connection to future events. It's easier to do so when the information is stark and extreme, and even more so when it's attached to strong emotions. That is why memories of very successful or painful experiences often define our memories of our past experiences.

The mind struggles with ambiguity, and that's why it tends to polarize experiences and predictions. It's this polarization of good and bad in the mind that creates anxiety and a fear of the future. The problem in sports, however, is that with most experiences, too much is unknown. The information simply can't be categorized with an all-or-nothing, win-or-lose mentality every single time. Sports psychologists and mental coaches have tried for years to prove that being process-oriented takes the pressure away from outcomes, even though outcomes are something that we can never really control anyway. It is only when the ambiguity is accepted as a standard does the athlete grow.

As you experience more of the unknown and are forced to sacrifice control of the outcome, you may actually start experiencing more angst and anxiety. It's easier for the mind to function when things are framed in a binary fashion: good or evil, win or lose, all or nothing. When you get to a place of ambiguity and certainty, the mind searches for reality and consistency, but the only known is the present, not the future. The challenge is that the present can become more anxiety provoking because the future is still on the horizon.

Every athlete prepares with the future in mind. There is a desire and a dream to make the future better than the past, and this can make it easy to overlook the present. The future will be – has to be – a different experience than where you are now. You may fall into the trap of making "What If" statements, but the future is always unknown. We can do everything in our power to try to control the future, but that's simply not going to create any real certainty. And in fact, the uncertainty of the future can become even more problematic when the mind tries to over-control each factor in an effort to better predict that future.

When this happens, the mind exhausts itself and lowers its defenses, which just opens the door for more and more anxiety to take over. We have to realize that fear, doubt, and insecurity is normal. Every elite athlete with whom I've ever worked has had fears about the future, doubts about their ability, and insecurity about their self-image. It's the degree to which each of these impact their preparation and outlook that defines their success and failure in competition.

Self-image is very important to an athlete, and to people in general. It's at the core of who we are, and it sets the stage for every one of our external and internal actions, from self-talk to our resiliency and grit and our ability to overcome challenges in the environment. Our self-image is also dynamic – it fluctuates up and down based on circumstances, feelings, and, sometimes, just randomness.

There are times in competition and life when we feel as though we're on top of the world. Perhaps you've overcome some really significant challenges or reached a certain level of success, and your confidence in your self-image begins to soar to an all-time high. You feel like a giant – strong, powerful, and excited. That's great, but unfortunately, that feeling tends to erode over time.

The erosion starts long before the destruction occurs. It starts with little planted ideas and thoughts that pop into our heads when we're unable to process effectively. Most athletes try to push these thoughts out of the consciousness and simply hope that they won't return, but those doubts are real. The insecurity is real – it's normal, and it's who you are. Your self-image is fueled by your ability to recognize doubts and insecurities and to focus on what you're capable of. As your self-image shifts and moves, it's always influenced by internal and external interactions.

Our internal interactions impact our self-image by identifying and processing information and seeing how it jibes with our perception of ourselves. Our own self-perception isn't always accurate, and in fact it's usually somewhat less flattering than how people actually see us. Our self-image, and our confidence in ourselves, is fluid. Through our interactions and our challenges we gain confidence and lose confidence as though we were making deposits and withdrawals from a large bank account. The goal is to make more deposits than withdrawals, but that's often easier said than done.

Our interaction with the external world also poses some challenges. We obviously never want the external world to take control of our internal belief systems, but our interactions with outside challenges can absolutely help reinforce and develop our internal resiliency-our belief in our ability to overcome challenges. It is through those internal and external interactions that our self-image, though fluid and dynamic, becomes crystallized.

That crystallized self-image is exactly what we need to avert the "What Ifs." "What If" questions are often based on fear avoidance – we try to manipulate the outcome to prevent bad things from happening. "What's the worst that could happen?" is a logical question. Unfortunately, until it's asked, the worst thing that could happen is usually the thing we fear the most. For most athletes, the biggest fear isn't losing a big game, it's having their own internal insecurities confirmed as true.

For every great athlete with whom I've worked, the fear that they may let down their teammates or not live up to their own belief systems is a strong one. But the more we get caught up in "What If" statements, the more we feed our doubts. There are no reassurances that will effectively alleviate insecurity or a doubt. Nobody can tell you how great you are enough times to make you believe that you're great. No one can reinforce the security of the challenge, any more than they can alleviate the doubts you're having about your chances for success or failure.

16

The Mountain of Belief
and a Cloud of Doubt

Every year, nearly one thousand climbers embark on professionally guided expeditions to the summit of the highest mountain in the world: Nepal's Mt. Everest. At approximately 29,000 feet, the peak of the mountain sits on top of the world, and since the 1920s has attracted climbers from around the globe.[13]

Mount Everest's "Death Zone" challenges even the fittest and most committed climbers in the world. It's unrelenting, and it doesn't discriminate. Even more sobering is that evidence of the zone's lethal nature remains for others to see as they pass through the zone on the way to the summit.

Kent Stewart, a Birmingham, Alabama, business owner, has attempted to summit Mt. Everest on four separate occasions. He shared with me his experiences and the challenges of climbing a mountain while facing death and the systematic breakdown of the human body. Stewart chronicled the mental and physical preparation needed for the climb – it's a trek that, once on the ground in Nepal, can take up to nine weeks, much of which is simply used to allow the body and mind to acclimate to the punishing altitude. Trying to go too fast on this climb is to risk almost certain death.

Everest is not for beginners; to prepare for the mountain, most climbers have already successfully conquered six other major summits around the world. As the tallest and most difficult mountain of all, Everest is often the final summit and the ultimate goal of many climbers. To prepare himself, Stewart begins physical training approximately nine months before leaving for the Himalayas, putting his body through various difficult physical challenges, including hours and hours on a StairMaster with a 40-pound pack strapped to his back, an approximate simulation of the demands he'll face while dressed in full climbing gear. "In a six-hour training session, the stairs never stop moving," he explains.

Once on the ground in Nepal, the climbing party makes an eleven-mile journey through small villages and across beautiful terrain – and entirely in the shadow of the mountain – to base camp. Once there, the climbers take more time to recharge and acclimate their bodies even more to the altitude. Over the next few weeks, the group will set out from base camp on a number of shorter climbs, ascending and descending to build up the stamina needed to operate in the region's thin air. Although shorter in distance and duration, these preparatory climbs require the men and women to successfully navigate the most dangerous region of the mountain: the Khumbu Icefall, right outside base camp. The Icefall is comprised of a glacier that bridges stable ground, and with each ascent to other camps on the mountain, climbers must guard against the avalanches, falls, and accidents common to this treacherous region. Danger on the mountain is never tomorrow – it's always today.

The "Death Zone" lies approximately 10,000 feet above the Khumbu Icefall, which itself sits at nearly 18,000 feet. As climbers begin their final ascent to the summit, they leave Camp Four – at roughly the 26,000-foot mark – in the middle of the night. Most climbers carry portable oxygen to counteract high-altitude oxygen depletion, but as the final push begins, everyone who has reached this point understands the ever-present risk of death, thanks to the punishment that their bodies are taking – from dehydration, exhaustion and high-altitude sickness – and the well-documented stories of those who perished before them.

The mortality risk on Mt. Everest has been estimated to be around four percent, and the Death Zone accounts for many of those fatalities, some of which involved climbers on their way up and others that took place during their descent. Unfortunately, due to the logistical difficulties of removing the dead from the mountain, the bodies of many of those who perish simply freeze and mummify in plain sight, often for decades, gruesome reminders of the mountain's fearsome power.

In 2015, Rachel Nuwar[14] published a harrowing account of the dangers of the Death Zone, in which she profiled one of its most famous victims, a 28-year-old Indian climber named Tseweng Paljor, known more familiarly by those passing through the zone as "Green Boots." Paljor died in a 1996 expedition, and other climbers must now pass his lifeless body – still shod in the bright green hiking boots he was wearing at the time – on their way to the summit. (It's apparently possible to see the sun's reflection off the boots from some of the lower camps.) Those boots and Paljor's final resting place on the mountain (along with the remains of scores of other unlucky climbers) serve as stark reminders of the harsh, unforgiving conditions faced by the men and women who continue to challenge the peak to this day.

In 2008, a group of researchers[15] undertook a study of the fatalities on Mt. Everest deaths to get a sense of why so many climbers in otherwise elite shape have succumbed to the conditions. They found that the leading cause of death, outside of accidents beyond the climbers' control, was high-altitude cerebral edema, a swelling of the brain due to the limited availability of oxygen at that altitude. The condition affects decision-making and ultimately causes a loss of physical coordination.

Victims such as Green Boots plant the seeds of doubt that climbers such as Stewart must fight every day on the mountain. No climber starts this kind of journey without a passionately strong belief that he or she can successfully reach the summit. These people are in their prime and in the best physical shape of their lives, but the reminders of the very real dangers of climbing and the temptation to quit threaten their success every step of the way. The only way these climbers can reach their goal is to balance their doubts with their beliefs and desires.

In the same way, every athlete with whom I work with must learn to balance their doubts and their beliefs. There isn't a single challenge or journey worth doing that doesn't become infected with doubts at some point. If you lack doubts, you're probably not pushing yourself on to more difficult challenges.

Doubts are normal. As the intensity of the task at hand increases, they rise from deep in your subconscious to challenge your purpose and intent. In much the way that water always manages to find a crack in the foundation of a house, doubts always manage to worm their way into your consciousness to expose the feared weaknesses within. When water pressure increases, the foundation cracks become larger; when competition pressure increases, your doubts and fears become larger. It's imperative that athletes of all levels learn to balance the doubt clouds.

Doubt will continue to search until it finds truth, and the mind will search and wander until it identifies the source of its own concerns. As doubt finds more and more needs, it also finds more and more reasons to believe that the doubts are accurate. To an actively engaged mindset, doubt is a healthy challenge, but to those with a weak self-image, it can be a recipe for disaster.

Doubt can impact you in two ways – through discipline or through derailment. Let me explain the latter first.

When faced with doubt in competition or training, you have the choice to believe or disbelieve the doubt. Since most of the doubt that you experience has some truth behind it, completely ignoring the insecurities that have bubbled up from the subconscious can be difficult. Questions about success come all the time, especially to the climbers who are pushing to reach the top. As Kent Stewart told me, the hardest thing about climbing a mountain isn't the physical abuse, but rather, the need to manage the doubts that continually arise during the climb. From lonely, freezing nights in a tent to those moments when the body and mind just seem to break down, doubts run rampant. For many climbers, those doubts – combined with the stark, physical reminders of death on display in the mummified corpses of Green Boots and others – make it easier to abandon the plan and turn back than to summon the strength within and draw on the training and preparation that got them there in the first place.

We saw the same thing in the Learning Curve section earlier in this book – changing course and starting over is easier than staying the path and pushing through. And doubt is the primary reason why people change course. Doubt grows like a weed, and when it's not met with any resistance, it takes over. But having doubts isn't a sign of mental weakness; on the contrary, it's completely normal to live in a world of doubt. To doubt is human. It's what you do about the doubt that separates those who thrive from those who merely survive.

The people who thrive engage the doubt and understand that it's a normal part of the human struggle. They turn doubt into discipline. Discipline is the desire to do what is asked, and to do it without compromise. Doubt usually comes with some angst and anxiety, which, if funneled in the appropriate direction, can actually keep you on task longer. Every great athlete must make sacrifices to be great. That sacrifice is built on discipline, not on doing what other people think you should do. It's doing what you believe you need to do, and doing it over and over and over again.

The mere presence of doubt is a reminder that more work can be done to improve, not that you're not capable of succeeding. Life and sport are lifelong learning environments, and continuous improvement is necessary. What is important is to be disciplined and stick with the plan and process of improvement. Elite performers use doubt to fuel discipline.

Stewart shared with me a great strategy that he and other climbers, as well as long-distance runners and endurance athletes, use when doubt arises on the mountain. When in a cloud of doubt, he said, try to discipline yourself to focus on the next two minutes of activity. Accept that your mind is filled with doubt, but be fully focused on what is being demanded of you. As your mind focuses on the task at hand and not the validation of your training and the probability of long-term success, it will move through the cloud of doubt.

For an athlete in training who is approaching an upcoming competition, doubt can fuel the discipline needed to get into the gym, get focused in practice, and get motivated through difficulty. The most important concern should be mastering the task at hand, not falling prey to the negativity brought on by the doubt and trying to fix problems. Getting disciplined to the challenge at hand strengthens the process. It has to be an internal choice that fuels your ability to transform the doubt into action.

As a competition draws near, fears, doubts, and insecurities rise. They rise because the mind starts to challenge the foundations that have been built through preparation and training. But doubts are not always accurate, but in that moment, the reality and accuracy of doubts are often thrown out the window in favor of increased anxiety and fear about not being prepared. The fact that doubts are rising is not the problem, as that is normal. It is failing to appreciate and know that your preparation is sufficient is the culprit.

When doubt fuels discipline it leads to execution and results. Few athletes have ever been truly confident in their process and their outcomes, and those who tend to get a little overconfident are quickly humbled by the game. Expectations rise, focus relaxes, and outcomes turn against you. It's the beauty of sports. If you let down your guard once you feel confident and your self-image has been enhanced, the game will humble you. Discipline is staying focused on your process, regardless of how many times you win and you achieve your goals. The best simply keep moving.

The best understand that doubts, fears, and insecurities are normal, but work to enhance their underlying self-image each and every day. The power of doubt and uncertainty is not in the feeling itself, it is in the resolution and acceptance of what those feelings mean. When we feel doubt, uncertainty, insecurity, and fear, the key is to try to understand why we feel that way. It's not necessary to search for the reasons we feel the way we do, just to understand where those feelings are coming from. That's the big distinction.

To overcome doubt, it's important to build a mountain of belief. An insurmountable force that you can use to face and overcome all challenges.

Doubt can only be overcome through belief. It can't happen any other way. A good outing, a special day, or a coach telling you that you've figured it all out won't help you overcome doubt. The only way is through relentless preparation, consistent effort, and purposeful investment in your performance. Those are the things that build belief.

Your belief won't grow by simply surviving challenges, unless you want to simply believe you can survive. Belief is only built by what you invest in yourself. Regardless of the challenge, the voice in your head is either an opponent (doubt) or a teammate (belief), and it will be your companion throughout the challenge. It's about investment.

Training and preparation are investments. When in competition, it is important that players draw on those past investments, not just hope that they'll show up. This is exactly why the need to validate is so dangerous. If the athlete is trying to validate the quality or quantity of past training, he or she is no longer competing in the present moment.

It's important to trust that the training will be implemented, not forced or purposefully recalled at the right moment.

In the heat of the moment, you want to trust the work that has been invested in – not borrowed against – your potential, your teammates, or the game itself. It's about drawing on your past to believe in your readiness to compete in the present. Once you understand that, the need to recall or validate the past is eliminated. The investment is realized through enhanced belief.

Belief is grown and nurtured through awareness of the investments and a desire to grow beyond the present moment. Instead of wasting energy in competition and training on all the potentially adverse outcomes that doubt might produce, invest that energy on being actively engaged in the challenge. Just like the climbers on Mt. Everest, all you can do in that moment is to trust your training and commit to the next two minutes of execution. It's not about getting over the doubts, but moving through them. Build that mountain of belief and never back away from an opportunity again.

Here's the question: Do you know what's really behind the doubts and belief? Most don't, because instead of learning, they allow doubts to derail the process, which in turn forces them to continually abandon their course of action. Learning is stunted, and painful experiences are repeated.

The goal is to smother doubt with belief. Absolutely smother it beyond recognition. It's not realistic to think that doubts won't occur and that belief will sustain. Every great athlete experiences doubts and struggles, often with a dangerous doubt-to-belief ratio in which the doubts simply overwhelm the belief.

For most athletes, doubts generally occur as the player reaches different levels on the journey to their goals. That's why climbers on Mt. Everest work their way through a variety of smaller climbs – they need to allow their body and brain to acclimate to the high altitude. As athletes approach new challenges, doubt is normal and to be expected. In this sense, it's a positive sign. For those athletes who live with absolute full mental engagement, the doubt fuels their discipline to challenge and overcome.

Doubt is so normal that many elite athletes struggle without it. In fact, some of them purposely create doubt to help drive their discipline and motivation. Coaches have been making negative comments about their teams in the media for years, displaying public doubt about the ability or the courage or the motivation of their players just to get them angry and ready to compete. It's an old trick, but it works so well that coaches go to the well and use it over and over again.

When you find yourself in a scenario in which doubts outnumber beliefs, try the following:

1. **Assess:** Take an inventory of your doubts and see which ones you actually believe. Seriously, take a piece of paper and write "Doubts" at the top of one side and "Beliefs" at the top of the other. Take some time and list them. The insights you'll glean will be amazing, not just from writing down the doubts but from listing the things that you actually believe about yourself.

   Take a look at the doubts and the themes that are highlighted by this exercise. These are the underlying insecurities that challenge you on a daily basis. This isn't meant to highlight your weaknesses, just to show that your doubts are often inaccurate, that they're often nothing more than those childhood monsters in your closet. Remember them? They were so mean, so ugly, and so dangerous, but only because you couldn't see them, it was the middle of the night, and no one could save you. Once you turned on the light, you discovered that the mean monster was actually Fluffy, your stuffed animal. Fluffy wasn't quite as dangerous as you had tricked your mind to believe he was.

2. **Accept vs. Fight:** Every athlete who competes experiences doubt. EVERY. SINGLE. ATHLETE. No one is immune. The best of the best, however, accept that their doubts are normal and then use them to make themselves better.

   Be careful not to look at others and assume that they're confident or free from doubt. They don't have thought bubbles over their heads, so stop trying to read the tea leaves to figure them out.

The Mountain of Belief and a Cloud of Doubt

You can't, so don't try. In a high-doubt mental environment, the things you overvalue as strengths in others are usually the things in yourself in which you lack confidence.

Accept that the presence of doubt means that you're normal, not mentally weak. Accept that there is a plan in place in the presence of doubt, and persevere through it. See the doubts as a sign that your competitive intensity is picking up, not that you're flawed or not ready. Quite the opposite. You're human. You're an athlete.

3. **Reset the Challenge:** The ability of the mind to take information and reframe it for an upcoming action is powerful. It should be said without hesitation that reframing a situation is a skill, not an innate ability. It takes maturity, experience, and awareness to reframe negative and challenging experiences into constructive engagements.

When doubts rise beyond the level of belief, simply reframing the experience can do wonders. It's similar to the discussion earlier about anxiety and adrenaline. Both are forms of arousal; where they differ is in how they relate to the current environment. Risky situations signal a threat and result in physical and mental feelings of anxiety, while excitement is often accompanied by an adrenaline rush. Feeling the arousal and reframing the situation, regardless of how difficult that might be, is a sign of a mentally strong person and athlete.

The only way to learn to reframe the challenge is to get comfortable in the challenge. I know that when I do exercises that have high heart-rate demands, I get really uncomfortable and start to restrict my effort. I just don't like the feeling. However, if I look at the challenge differently and count the reps backwards, my effort always surges. The change is a mental one – my body didn't do anything differently.

Reframe the doubts as reminders to get disciplined for the challenge and the plan that's been created. It's about believing that you're capable in that moment.

4. **Engage:** Every challenge requires your full attention and effort. If it doesn't demand that of you, it's not difficult or important enough to make you give everything you have in your tank.

You don't need an invitation to compete; all that's needed is an opportunity.

When doubts start to build, the common mindset is to avoid, back off, and start rebuilding the necessary skillsets and fixing the problems that prompted the doubt. That's the worst thing you can do, because it becomes a repetitive process. As doubts increase and challenges are avoided, more doubts build up. There is a never a "better" day to compete, because there are no guarantees that those days will actually be any better. The only way to push through your doubts is to run through them with the aggressiveness and competitiveness that you have deep within your mindset. Engage the moment and push through the challenge. Your behavior is fueled by your mindset, so a mindset of doubt will create protective and fearful behavior – in other words, exactly what you fear. If your mindset is about engagement and fighting through the doubts with the beliefs you have in yourself – even if it's just one belief – that's infinitely better than dwelling on the ten things you doubt about yourself.

Think about prizefighters. As they walk to the ring, the months of grueling training are behind them. This isn't the time for them to worry about whether they've trained appropriately, particularly when it comes to readiness, fitness, and strategy. All that will do is distract them from the fight itself. As long as they know that they fully followed their training plan, those doubts will disappear as they step into the ring. Now is the time for them to focus fully on the strengths and advantages that they have in the fight, and to believe in them fully. That's the only choice, and the only choice of champions.

Belief is why champions are champions.

17

The Struggle of Competition

It doesn't matter if you're a Hall of Famer or a someone who never reached their true potential – without question, the struggle is coming. That's guaranteed. The great ones understand that the struggle of competition, the struggle of life, and often the fear of their own athletic mortality are checkpoints in the journey to excellence, not destinations.

Success often cycles through the good and the bad, usually without any predictive rhythm as to why. If you look at seasons in which an athlete has enjoyed immense success, there are great things that the athlete and coach were able to control and influence that contributed to that success. On the flip side, when the struggle arrives, there are often plenty of things outside everyone's control that result in great difficulty. Struggles aren't always self-inflicted, just as success isn't always self-created.

That's an important distinction. It's very easy to take complete ownership when things are going well. The good breaks, the great opportunities, and the good fortune that comes your way isn't always in your control. In sports, an inch can turn a season from good to great or good to horrendous. That inch can mean the difference between a fair or foul ball; a putt falling into the hole or rolling ten feet past; or a football player making a great catch with his foot just inbounds – or just out of bounds. An inch between good and great.

Does this inch really wield that much control over the ultimate outcome? Absolutely not. Over the course of any game, match, or tournament, an overlooked play early in the competition – a shot on the fifth hole of the second round, for example, or an offensive drive in the second quarter of a football game – may very well have a greater impact on the outcome, but few people understand that. Why? Because the early moment isn't as emphasized or intense as the critical moment at the end.

So when an athlete highlights the struggles of his or her season, there is so much more to it for me. There are significant lessons that must be understood. It can be a very confusing experience for an athlete to deemphasize the current successes or struggles and instead focus on the "keystone" events that occurred much earlier in competition. If a golfer had made that four-foot putt in the middle of the second round, for example, the winning margin would have been larger at the end of the tournament. If a basketball player had made those two free throws at the ten-minute mark of the first half, the two-point lead with the heightened pressure at the end of the game might have been more comfortable, just as a two-possession game in football is always different than a tight contest that features a last-possession opportunity to win the game.

Even more significant than the early successes are the early struggles and how the athlete, coach, or team manages the psychological impact of those struggles. When an athlete is enjoying a stretch of great play, the struggles are often overlooked and treated simply as focus points that the player can use to reconnect to their process. But when an athlete is struggling, the things that go wrong are no longer focus points, just a reflection of whatever's wrong with their game, their plan, or their approach. It becomes so much more, and that's a devastating trap.

The little differences between good and great and good and bad are often simply a matter of how the athlete sees them. Highly confident athletes see struggles as part of the process. Insecure athletes see struggles as impending doom.

Back in the pioneer days, farming was the lifeblood. Every year, the farmers would plant their crops and invest their entire lives into the success of those crops. Not only did their families rely on the bounty of the crop, so did the entire community. Farming takes a tremendous amount of trust. After a farmer plows the field and prepares the soil for planting, there's a significant amount of time between the seeds going into the ground and the harvest. A lot of variables can influence the health, growth, and ripening of the crop, and most of these are out of the farmer's control.

After planting, the farmer simply fertilizes and waits. He must wait for actions to occur below the surface, out of sight. Seed after seed must simply go through its own process. Not all of them grow, but that's why the farmer plants so many of them. The trust and the planning must be invested in.

Fertilizer is the key, in my opinion. After planting, the only thing the farmer can do is provide the appropriate nutrients to the environment to stimulate the growth of the crop. The complex chemical makeup of the fertilizers available today is a scientific miracle, and much like these highly specialized and strategic agricultural products, the advancements being made today in the athletics and performance-improvement field dwarf the efforts of the past.

Long before fertilizer became a highly refined, complex chain of chemicals, farmers fertilized their crops with the manure produced by their livestock. Manure may not be pleasant, but it's a powerful fertilizer and was the go-to solution for farmers for thousands of years. So we might say that for growth to occur, success had to push through layers of crap.

Sounds like sports, right? For every success, there are deep layers of struggle, difficulty, and disappointment, all of which help fertilize long-term success.

Life is no different. I see many individuals who are afraid to keep a daily record of their training sessions and the progress they've made, and many others who simply refuse to look in the mirror to understand what went well and what didn't. This is troublesome to me. How can you learn if you don't evaluate your successes and failures on a daily basis?

If you're too afraid to look with a discerning mindset at the mistakes you've made in life, then all you're doing is burying your head in the sand. Life is about learning. It's simple, really. We must learn, from experience to experience, to gain the wisdom to make a better life moving forward.

One of the hardest things to manage in my role as a clinical and sports psychologist is to deal with the struggle and pain of those who seek my services. I can feel the distress they're in. Very few contract with me without some sort of conflict going on, whether they're trying to overcome a challenge or learning something new to help them work through a growth period. It's the nature of the business, but I'm human, and I often find myself thinking and worrying about the progress that my clients are (or aren't) making. My interest in them and their success keeps me engaged in everything I do.

Unfortunately, as much as we might prepare for greatness, the true essence of who we are is defined in life's struggles, not its glory. The pain and frustration of the struggle is necessary for growth and learning, but it still hurts, challenges, and confuses us. The dynamic nature of life is about the wholeness and the struggle and the balance between the two of them.

It may seem important to understand why we struggle. Throughout my early Catholic education, every religion, every search for faith, and every story of redemption starts with a struggle, and through this struggle comes enlightenment. According to the teachings of the Buddha, life is about struggle and the enlightenment that comes from accepting that the struggle is real, it has a reason and a cause, and it has an end. Only through understanding struggle can the pathway to wholeness be found, and once it's found, the cycle continues.

Luke Skywalker in the *Star Wars* movies had to work through his own doubts, struggles, and insecurities to understand the power of The Force. Through his struggle, and because he questioned himself and his teachers along the way, The Force became powerful. This is basically how it works for any process of growth and development. Learning, confusion, and frustration are all critical if we want to shine the light on the mastery that we all desire. Struggle never goes away; it just waits in the background until you need a lesson in life. Unfortunately, the process of struggling is self-fertilizing – the more emotional energy you provide, the greater the struggle.

Since we can accept that struggles are an essential experience of life, it's important to understand that the mentality maintained and the effort made during the struggle is critical. What do we do in a struggle? Sometimes too much – what you try to do may actually keep you struggling longer than if you had done nothing. That's not to say that "do nothing" is an acceptable mental technique, because I feel that that advice is one of the most reckless and destructive "recommendations" that a mental coach can give to a client. Telling a client to do nothing is like telling him or her to read harder, concentrate more, or try harder to fall asleep. It's not what you try that's the problem; it's how hard you try it.

When you struggle, the mind often becomes cluttered and motivated by the desire to get out of and simply survive the struggle. A struggle hurts, and it tends to turn one's senses, thoughts, and actions toward simply trying to get out of the struggle. Much like what happens when a building is evacuated and everyone tries to get out as quickly as possible, the goal when struggling is to get to safety and serenity, and not necessarily in a safe fashion. That desire to escape enlists every protective mechanism in the body and the mind, and over time, tends to wear down the protective defenses and other important resources. The harder things get, the more you become desperate to find external solutions, quick fixes, strategies that worked for your friends, more sleep, less sleep, and so on – all of which results in more and more clutter and confusion. After a while, you're completely exhausted, but only because you were trying to do everything you could. The harder you try, the worse it gets. The problem isn't the strategies or tools, external answers, or activities, but the motivations and mindset behind them. When you're just trying to survive, things look a lot different than when you're learning, persevering, and moving forward.

When you're struggling in life, sport, business, or relationships, remember that you're the most valuable contributor of your own pathway to success and mastery. The vast majority of the time (because I know there is that one reader who will say "but in this circumstance it could"), the struggles you experience won't kill or destroy you. You have the ability to rebuild and persevere. It may not be easy, may not be in the timeframe that you desire, and may not happen according to your plans, but every dusk has a dawn. You're ultimately in control of your destiny, and accepting that mindset can empower you.

Here are a couple of points that you should understand about working through a struggle:

1. The Struggle Will End...Eventually:

No one really knows when, but it will end. After every dark night comes the sunrise. However, if you doubt that better days are ahead or you worry about the difficulty of today, you will miss the growth and glory of the day. When you get so worried about what may happen, you miss what is happening. Understand that no matter how bad things get, there will be an end and a rebirth. The most important thing is to separate your self-belief and self-identity from the struggle. You may be having a very difficult time, but you're not a failure, or someone who's destined for difficulties, cursed, or followed by a black cloud. You're a human being with an opportunity to define and determine your ultimate destiny, and the struggle can help you with that.

2. The Most Powerful Thing You Can Do Is ACCEPT:

Accept that you're struggling, accept yourself, and accept that you can work your way through it. Too many people romanticize the idea of their future selves and try to relive or overwrite the past, and this usually results in a failure to accept who and what you are right now. It may be painful and scary to accept what you are right now, but it's a critically important factor as you try to move through a struggle. Look in the mirror and learn to accept who you are right now. You are what you are, good or bad; it's only you looking back in the mirror. Learn to accept that the struggles of today cannot destroy you unless you allow them to by devaluing yourself, giving more emotional power to the struggles, or giving up.

3. The Harder You Try, the Worse It Gets:

Have you ever tried to run uphill on ice? The harder and faster you try, the sooner you'll fall. The natural instinct is to try harder. In fact, I have developed and published articles on the concept of the "RipTide" – those times when life suddenly turns on you. People forget to breathe, forget to take account of current resources, and forget to slow the mind down by focusing on the present moment. There are pathways that you can use to work through the struggle, but if you're all worked up and trying to find the immediate answer RIGHT NOW, you're not using your ability to persevere. Take a deep breath and allow yourself to experience a little bit of the stress and angst of the struggle. It won't kill you.

4. **Resist the Urge to Only Search for External Solutions:**

Such tools and skills can be helpful, but the true answer is the mindset behind the solutions. In other words, if you're searching for a new mental trick, or an answer from an expert, a friend, or your favorite author, you're abandoning the mindset of accepting yourself in favor of a quick fix. You hold the answer, so it's time to listen to that mindset of acceptance and perseverance.

5. **Struggles Are the Greatest Lessons You Can Ever Experience in Life:**

I believe that struggles exist for a reason: to allow us to learn more about ourselves and to teach us how to succeed in life. Without challenges, learning is slower and less impactful. If you think about your life, some of the greatest lessons you've ever learned took place during times that were probably the most difficult for you. If you look for quick fixes and avoid the process of working through the struggle, the struggle will eventually return, but this time, it'll probably be harder and more intense. It's more productive to just accept that you have to learn through it and then embrace the journey.

6. **You're Not Failing Because You're Struggling:**

Everyone struggles, but those who embrace the power of knowing who they are and what they embody are the ones who grow through struggles. What's important is that you don't compare yourself to others. Making comparisons is human nature, but understand that you only compare and evaluate yourself on those factors that you perceive to be weaknesses in you and strengths in others. Remember, acceptance is important – it's where you start to build a pathway through your struggles.

It is hard to put a ribbon on the pain of personal, emotional, or relationship struggles, but the truth is that because of the outsider's perspective I have with my clients, it's often just necessary to encourage persistence rather than a quick fix. The power that each of you has is your ability to succeed through any circumstances and to create the future you desire. Start by understanding how struggles impact you and influence your mindset, and then learn to see them differently. In the end, only one question matters: "How can I be the best, most authentic person I can be?"

Building
Your
Manifesto

"To truly realize your potential in sports and life, it all begins in the mind. It starts with a belief and a desire to achieve what you dream of achieving. Only when you invest in your thinking does your thinking transform into positive and successful action. Those who reach their goals know before they achieve them because they have dreamt about it, visualized it, and invested fully in achieving it. From those desires originate determination."

– Dr. Bhrett McCabe

18

The MindSet of Getting
It Done - Whenever, However

Talent, ability, and technical skills can only take you so far. No matter how good you are now or how much success you've had in the past, there will come a time when talent can't overcome the underlying limitations in your game.

I see this all the time. An athlete moves through the younger and less experienced levels of competition and builds confidence in their ability. In competition, they look like monsters, running roughshod over the other players and doing so with an ease of execution that gets coaches, fans, scouts, and recruiters excited.

So how do these athletes fail to progress when they move to the next level? How can they be "can't miss" athletes one year and fail to advance to the level of their expectations the next? Most of the time, the talent disparity eventually narrows and the gaps in the early-starter's process, approach, and, most importantly, mindset leave them exposed and unsuccessful.

A mindset is the climate of the athlete – it serves as his or her underlying perspective and approach. It can be developed and controlled. Unlike outcomes, the mindset is the factor that separates the great athletes from the norm. The application of that mindset each day is like the weather – it is influenced by the climate and expressed on that day. Unlike outcomes, the mindset is the factor that separates the great athletes from the norm.

The MindSide Manifesto

Unlike the mindset, you can never control outcomes. You can influence them and try to increase the odds of them working in your favor, but you can never guarantee or determine an outcome. All you can control is effort, preparation, intensity, your desire to compete, and your resiliency.

If you *could* control outcomes, would you really enjoy competition as much? No, you'd most likely become bored. Think about it this way. Every day, the sun rises in the east and sets in the west. But the only time most people pay attention to these two natural events is when they happen to be outside in some kind of unusually dramatic location, like a mountain or a beach. On most other days, you probably don't pay much attention them, because they're commonplace and predictable.

When athletes and people try to control outcomes, what they're really trying to do is limit exposure to the things in their lives that they fear, the true monsters in the closet. We all have fears, doubts, and insecurities. For far too many of us, the competitive landscape isn't about achieving, but rather, about preventing outcomes that may confirm the deepest, darkest fears we have about ourselves.

What can be so bad that we actively try to work against it? Usually, we protect ourselves against the idea that we may actually be a fraud who's unable to succeed when it matters, and that everyone will now see that what we fear about ourselves is the truth. Through every iteration of success, we simply change the outcome demands to confirm our worth and value. It's never enough, the bar gets raised, and we change how we view ourselves.

I have an athlete who summarizes it perfectly. He's a discus thrower who has struggled in the past with inconsistent performances and growing during the course of the season. After working together he told me he gets it now, that he needs to "Create, Don't Imitate" every day. For far too long he had tried to continue to reach the outcomes that he defined as being good enough to compete at an elite level with world-ranking capabilities. So he entered every weight session, every throwing session, and every training review with the idea that he would not imitate past results, something that created significant stress in the past. When he tried to imitate the past, he never thought about going beyond, but instead, just tried to meet a standard that would show that he was consistent and not losing ground. It became a struggle for him.

We changed his perception to one of creating magic daily, regardless of what he has left in his mental and physical tank. By creating and not imitating, he has changed his mentality to bring forth what he's capable of that day, to take advantage of his capacity to perform. Ultimately, it was about accepting that a good or bad day didn't change his ability to compete the following day. We bring different feels and abilities to the playing field each day, so make the most of those days and maximize your capacity.

The best of the best possess a mindset that allows them to achieve their greatness, and from that they build their plan to achieve their goal. It always starts with a mindset. It's never by accident, always by design. This should come as no surprise and has been covered by numerous writers in the past — you need to invest in the process. At LSU, we had "the system." Everything we did, we did with full trust that the system that we had bought into was going to work for us. The system was everything – from how you planned practice, to when you had off-season meetings, to what the strategy was on a full count in the fifth inning. It was based on probabilities and executed with trust and commitment.

There is a process in place for building a championship mindset. It's rarely born, always developed. A competitive mindset always starts with a performance philosophy and is accompanied by a desire to do something. Mindsets always have a purpose. A runner never runs without a goal or destination in mind – they'd simply end up running in circles. The underlying philosophy and a purpose are the components of a mindset every single time. Unfortunately, few people realize that they have either. And finally, a mindset must have a plan to support it. A dream is simply a desire unless there's a plan to achieve it. Then it becomes a purpose.

The Performance Philosophy:

Do you have a performance philosophy? Most players and coaches don't spend the time to understand how they should engage in competition and training. The most common approach is to mimic the philosophy of a coach who's had the largest impact on you, or a player who acted as a mentor for you. Understanding tendencies and how your mind sees competition is critical when developing plans and strategies. Without a strategy, the mind is left to attach itself to any influence it desires. That's a risk that I'm never comfortable taking.

I was sitting with a coach recently and I asked her what her philosophy was for coaching student-athletes. Her reply was pretty much what I expected, and that bothered me. She said that when she starts the year, she's looking for athletes who have great attitudes, work hard, and compete through both good and bad. She said that those factors consistently separate her successful teams from those that struggle.

The problem was, when I asked her what those attributes were, she said "Come on Doc, you know what I'm talking about!" I asked her if she was sure. I told her that my definitions might be a little different than hers – and I guaranteed her that her athlete's definitions would be significantly different than her own. The truth was that she was a very invested in each player at a personal level, knew the game inside and out, and was a tireless worker, among other attributes. But while they appeared rather obvious, her philosophy did not really match her attributes.

This is why it's easy to get frustrated when you're coaching your players and you see them struggle in certain aspects of the game – they're simply unsure what you're looking for. When your definitions match their definitions, the results will usually be great. But too many coaches don't clearly define their expectations, or the pillars of their coaching strategy, and then clearly communicate them to their team. And very often, the reason for that is that the coach has never really defined it for him- or herself.

To be an effective coach or player, you need to define exactly what you want, what you plan to work toward, and how to measure it. Imagine sending your home contractor to buy a door for the front of your house. Of course you want a great door, but would they define a "great door" the same way you would? Probably not. You have to give them specific dimensions and styling, or even an order number!

I would suggest that you split a piece of paper into two columns – one side for the physical expectations and the other side for the mental. As you list different aspects, come back and start cleaning it up, eliminating those that may be important but not as important than others, and those that may overlap with others. Then try to define each aspect.

For instance, if you're a golf coach, and one of the things you list in the physical column is that it's important to have an effective short game, what exactly does that mean? If you're a baseball coach, and you list the importance of being a good base runner, does that mean that the runner can effectively anticipate a ball in the gap and take the turn at second to make it to third? Or does it mean something else? As you can see, as you define things more and more precisely, you can start developing training and coaching plans to effectively train your team.

The same thing holds true for the mental aspects. If you've written that you want your players to be patient, how do you define that? Does it mean that if you're running late to a meeting they won't get upset? Of course not – you want someone who can stay focused on the process if things aren't going their way and who trusts that they'll be able to turn things around. Something like that can be trained. You can work, for example, on confusing your players in competition to see which athletes resist the need to respond emotionally and instead stick to their process, an attribute that for you as a coach is a much more useful definition of patience.

Too many athletes make up things as they go along, so to be successful, it's important to know what you want to improve and achieve, and to sacrifice every distraction and extraneous variable you can to succeed. Knowing specifically what you want and what your overall approach to achieving it will be is as important as anything else in your game. Success doesn't simply appear; it's created. Knowing your philosophy is the biggest step to getting there.

Purpose:

The greatest influence of a mindset is that it creates the purpose that motivates and drives the athlete. For each athlete, there is a drive inside that pushes them through the fears, doubts, and hard times.

In my opinion, Michael Jordan is the greatest basketball player to ever play the game. He redefined offense with his explosive movements around the court. In the first few seasons of his career, Jordan moved the game inches above the rim and away from the perimeter, and fans packed stadium after stadium to watch him play. His brand of basketball was fun and energetic.

I always found his mindset to be fascinating. Because he was the greatest player in the game, every other player on the court looked forward to playing against him, even though the outcome of the game and the challenge they faced were usually not in their favor.

When Jordan was elected to the Basketball Hall of Fame in 2009, his acceptance speech provided insight to his mindset, as categorized by Jon Greenberg.[16] Unfortunately, most writers and fans missed it because they were caught up in Jordan's delivery. As he took the stage, he spoke off the cuff and from his heart. He began to describe different people who inspired him throughout his career, from his junior days all the way to his final return from retirement. With each person he mentioned, it became clear that he had created a perspective that other players who were guarding him or competing against him didn't respect him or his game.

That was probably the furthest thing from the truth, but for Jordan, the anger of being disrespected had driven him to be the best. Over the course of his career, he would draw on statements made in the media or even create conflicts in his mind with opponents, just so he could focus on his purpose and mindset to beat them. His purpose wasn't what fans thought it was, but he still used it every time to drive his own greatness.

There are two men with whom I've had the pleasure of spending time and who have redefined purpose for me. Joshua Foster and Timothy Alexander share more than a life confined to a wheelchair. They share more than having seen their lives change in an instant due to an automobile accident. Today, both live prosperous lives because they chose to see their purpose in different ways.

Joshua Foster admitted that prior to his accident he was simply a man existing. Nothing was wrong and nothing was right. He was living to see each day progress, without much purpose or achievement. But the evening he ended up wrapped around a pole changed his life psychologically even more than physically.

Foster described lying in the hospital bed after doctors had told him that the spinal cord injury that severed his T-10 vertebrae would leave him with no feeling or movement below his waist. He hadn't been drinking and driving or being reckless. In fact, the car had been going about 25 miles per hour. Now, lying in that bed, his purpose became as clear as it had ever been in his life. He was going to train and become a bodybuilder.

Seventy-two hours after the accident, Foster locked in on a purpose to transform his life. Even though he was still in intense pain and under the influence of very strong painkillers, Foster saw physical training and weightlifting as a purpose – a way to be independent, an inspiration, and a competitor.

Three years after the accident, Foster won his professional debut as a figure, or physique, competitor. His body and mind had transformed to one of purpose and intent. No longer searching in life, the new Foster was focused on discipline, training, and breaking barriers. He's no longer dependent on his family. He's a personal trainer and a professional bodybuilder.

Timothy Alexander also sits in a wheelchair, also paralyzed. The morning after a high school football game in which he had delivered the game-winning block, Alexander found himself sitting in a burning car, unable to move. And the fact that he couldn't move was just the start. His journey would span nearly two years, during which he would battle infections, depression, and hopelessness.

Asking God for help, Alexander found the inspiration and purpose that he needed: to play college football. The problem, unfortunately, was that he was unable to move his legs and had limited movement in his torso. He wouldn't be able to physically play, even if he weren't confined to a wheelchair.

Through intense physical rehabilitation and vocational rehabilitation, Alexander started taking college courses at a local community college and succeeded. He became inspired enough to approach the new football coach at the University of Alabama-Birmingham and ask him for an opportunity. The coach, Garrick Magee, agreed on one condition: that he participate in all activities like every other player.

Alexander's purpose was to be a vital member of the team, but he had no idea the role he would eventually play. His purpose was fueled by the intent to work out with personal trainers to gain movement and strength in his torso, to attend every class and every 6:00 a.m. workout with his teammates. There would be no excuses.

After the 2014 season, despite the leadership of a new coach and an improved record on the field, UAB decided to discontinue the football, women's rifle and bowling programs as part of a cost-cutting effort. For a player who fought so hard to become part of the team, this was not a viable option. Alexander may not have been able to play on the field, but he never missed a snap mentally and provided much-needed encouragement to players who were suffering from the mental and physical punishment that football dishes out. Now more than ever, his purpose was clear.

Alexander, along with several other prominent alumni, began to hold rallies, plan meetings, and systematically organize the student body to fight for the UAB football program. For a student body that had not exactly flocked to the school's football games, this was a dramatic shift in support. So much so that the student body agreed to add a small fee to their tuition to pay for the return of all three sports. Alexander became the face of the movement, and he didn't stop until the mission was complete.

Foster and Alexander both embody a Determined Mindset. That type of mindset is fueled by a clear purpose to achieve an outcome. When the first goal is achieved, the purpose shifts to the next goal. There are no breaks, no rests.

A Determined Mindset understands what is capable because it often matches the person's overall philosophy toward success and competition. This isn't conjecture – the alignment between philosophy and purpose always leads to action. *Always.*

Unfortunately, too many athletes lack determination and purpose and instead compete from a Defeated Mindset. Allowing external factors to have power over their effort and purpose, those with a Defeated Mindset are quick to abandon a plan or process when factors don't align in their favor. They typically embody the fixed-mindset approach, because they fail to appreciate the impact that they can make in their own lives. So it's just easier for them to give in to the challenges than it is to face and overcome them.

Understanding your purpose requires you to know yourself and why you compete and train. It doesn't require a tragic or traumatic event to shine the light on your purpose. Find the factors that engage your mind fully, and trust why you're reacting with such energy and emotion to the challenge or cause. That's your purpose.

There is never a missing link to your purpose. The answer always lies in the burning desires that you hold deep down, never in suggestions or demands from those around you. Your underlying purpose is the most personal and vulnerable that you'll ever be. And as we know, that's when we're at our best.

The Plan and Process:

The plan and process is always bigger than the athlete and always more robust than the outcome. Since we can never control or guarantee an outcome, the emotional investments of worrying about outcomes are shifted to the energy and effort of the approach, the recipe, and the process of success.

Why do we prepare and practice?

There is nothing more important in a well-developed process than a practice plan. Unfortunately, in my opinion, when most athletes are in control of their own practice, they use it to fix and correct. They do that with the idea that if they can simply correct the problems that plagued them in the last competition or competitions, they'll find success. That's flawed thinking, which often originates from a defeated mindset and lacks a strong philosophy and purpose.

When athletes fail to lock into a purposeful plan, they assume that their success and successful mindset have already been determined, and that if they just do what they've been trying to do, but better, they'll be successful. In other words, success is about getting all of the pieces to line up together.

Furthermore, a lack of a definitive process assumes that the conditions for competition stay the same and the ability of all of the competitors also stays the same. Too many athletes think that fixing one problem fixes the model of performance, and that's just wrong.

The mindset of Fixing is different than the mindset of Mastery. I want my athletes to compete and train to mastery, so when they walk into the unknown nature of competition, they can do so safe in the knowledge that they'll be able to adjust and create success. Training to fix is result-avoidance – it's the fear that your problem has something to do with your ability, and that it thus must be fixed. As we've discussed elsewhere in the book, nothing successful arises out of a mentality of fixing.

Why do we talk about and invest so much in the process? The best of the best, athletes from across the board – Olympians, fighters, golfers, and national championship coaches – understand that the pathway is always more important than the destination, but it's through the pathway that the desired destination becomes reality. When there is stress in sport, the process shows us where to invest our energy.

What are the hallmarks of a process built to capitalize on the mindset of determination and purpose?

1. The process is determined prior to starting, and can be adjusted but not changed. It's developed with the purpose of succeeding, so the psychological investment into the plan is highest at the onset. The hard thing is to stick with it when time has passed, but to also understand that adjustments will have to be made. That's normal.

2. It's created based on strengths – and working on those strengths – to improve. Great teams and processes are always built around strengths. It makes no sense for a plan to be built to correct weaknesses and simply ignore the strengths. Businesses would never follow this model. In fact, large corporations eliminate underperforming divisions and recruit investors on their strengths.

3. Trust in the process during competition provides the ability to overcome weaknesses. When the pressure of competition mounts, the plan and process sustain, not fold.

4. Great processes incorporate every facet of the organization, not just the ones in the spotlight. The best work happens behind the scenes in activities that provide support for the overall mission. Years ago, I worked with a college basketball team that knew they were going to struggle with physical match-ups, but also knew that they could exploit other teams by trusting their system of video review and analysis. While not a direct, measureable aspect of the team's performance, this video system – developed by a young graduate student – won the players over, and through their trust, was able to give the team a competitive advantage that led the team to a successful season. Their process was unique, but they trusted it.

5. The process requires unrelenting commitment, and most players don't have the fortitude to stick with it. We live and compete in a

world of shortened attention spans, and it's often hard for young men and women to hold on for months before they see results. The younger the athlete, the shorter the attention span, so it's important that athletes and coaches resist any urge to abandon their process.

6.   It provides athletes with a cause bigger than themselves. When they buy into a process, they buy into a perceived advantage to succeed.

The hardest thing for an athlete to do is to stay patient with the process in the face of so many distractions and disappointments. Sacrifice and elite focus are vital to success. Knowing how success arises, where success arises from, and building a plan to achieve success defines the differences between those who are successful and those who are not.

If you think about the major Division I college football programs, there are more similarities than differences between the successful and unsuccessful programs. Every program has better facilities than they did twenty years ago, and the science of coaching elite athletes has improved so dramatically that essentially every coach has better coaching tools than their predecessors. Therefore, the factor that differentiates successful programs the most is the program's vision and the unrelenting commitment by the program to the factors that contribute to the successful implementation and execution of the plan to win. Those who consistently win simply do it better than everyone else. There's no magic – it's just sacrifice, effort, and a mindset on the part of everyone in the program to just get it done.

19

The Five Things That the Best Do Everyday

The great ones have a plan of action, a competitive philosophy, and a vision to achieve. Those are the easy things. Doing it is the hard part.

When studying the best of the best, in sports, the corporate world, and in life, there's always a series of predictable actions. What I never understand is why others don't adopt, implement, and learn from these leaders more. We always assume that success is simply this magical experience and forget the long hours, the tireless activities, and the hurts and pain that accompanies success.

Back in the trade-industry days, a young high school graduate would select a trade, such as carpentry or masonry. The goal wasn't to be an expert immediately, but to invest in the trade system so that when you became an expert, you carried a seal that represented hours and hours of work over years of training. To become a craftsman, a master, you learned every action from a master craftsman.

Unfortunately, today's young people are growing up in a world in which information is so readily available that expertise is perceived and not earned. We're riddled with self-proclaimed experts rather than those who work their way up the ladder and learn to wash their own tools and sharpen their own blades.

I receive e-mails almost every day from young psychologists and mental coaches asking me how to get into the industry and work with athletes. My answer is always the same: Check your pride at the door and learn from the best in the field in your region. Learn everything they do, from how they market their business to how they clean their office.

Rookies must do the same. In professional sports, rookies are often in much better physical shape than the older players, but they often lack the mental acuity to be successful.

Success is a process, never an accident. I think we've covered that topic a few times by now, but for many, the process is lacking.

There are five things the best of the best do every day:

1. Administrative Work:

It's important to address your administrative needs every day. These are the things that will take place in the next three weeks or so and thus require immediate attention, such as paying bills, booking flights, making appointments, and planning training. Too many people procrastinate in this area, and when it finally truly needs to be taken care of, they either panic or do it at the expense of something else. I recommend that you do this first thing in the morning, and that includes planning your day. Get the hassles out of the way when you have the most mental energy available.

As an athlete, you may look at the menial tasks associated with this step and just assume that they'll work themselves out. Huge mistake. Administrative demands tend to build up over the course of the day, but it's still easy to put them off. The problem, unfortunately, is that as these small stressors build, they become significant impairments to your overall mental makeup. The mental acuity and flexibility needed to meet the competitive demands of your sport are robbed from you. It's a little like running a racecar while pulling a trailer. Eventually the demands will rob your ability to push your mind and body to the limits. There won't be anything left in the tank.

Your morning list will allow you to get ahead of this. You might take an hour to book your flights, or to handle such tasks as planning your meals, organizing your practices, and coordinating with your team. There's no reason to assume that these things will take care of themselves, and in all honesty, they take more mental energy to avoid than they do to address. Get those minor hassles off your plate so you can free up additional mental energy.

Why the morning? That's typically when the mind is freshest and can act as more of an effective filter. There are also fewer distractions, and the day's activities have yet to pile up. As your important tasks drain your mental energy during the day, taking care of the little things becomes a lot less inviting. Getting these out of the way triggers a feeling of accomplishment, limits the distraction and dread of knowing that you failed to finish tasks, and frees up your mental working space to succeed as the day goes on.

2. **Developmental Tasks:**

With Administrative tasks focused on the smaller responsibilities that build up day-to-day, Developmental tasks are those that relate to longer-term ideas and needs, roughly three weeks to six months out. These tasks require your attention because progress and success can't be implemented unless you've planned for the future. There's a balance between planning, dreaming, and executing. These needs are about planning and getting the pieces in place so that when you're moving closer, it's no longer a fire drill but just some administrative follow-through. There's a big difference.

The ability to see the landscape is an important task. For athletes, who face difficult practices and the demands of daily competitions, it can be hard to look past the next day, but your coaches and support team are always thinking about the future and managing your training accordingly. Being able to see and plan for the future makes all the other activities collaborative and aligned to the ultimate goal. It's never efficient to run around as though your hair's on fire trying to fix problems that have arisen due to bad planning, so if you can get ahead of the demands of the next three months and plan efficiently, your success rate will increase.

What are some examples of an athlete's Developmental Tasks? Meetings with members of your support team, such as your psychologist, trainer, coach, and nutritionist, are great places to start, and you should have a plan in place for each discipline. As with all athletes, there is likely a goal and vision in mind, and putting the Developmental Tasks on your daily calendar will encourage the mind to organize and plan toward execution.

Developmental planning removes the clutter from your present consciousness because by effectively planning for the next few months, your mind is able to recruit and implement the tools it needs to succeed. Avoiding the Developmental tasks will simply put you behind the eight ball when it matters. Think of a business – without long-term planning, they'd function in a strictly reactionary world and end up more stressed and frustrated than they would have been if they had done the small daily Developmental planning tasks.

This step is no doubt hard for athletes. It's hard to commit to plans that are down the road. It's easy to talk about the future in romantic terms ("next year I'll be able to…"), but few really plan how to get there. The power of an athlete's mind is to think that they can achieve something without facing much resistance, but the truth is that as the competitive landscape continues to increase, this planning step becomes more and more powerful.

I'm often asked to work with teams on setting goals. In theory it's a great idea for coaches and players to set goals, but in reality they don't really work.

My experience is that the weekend seminars designed to develop goals, mission and vision statements take away from the effort and energy of achieving them. I'm not saying that they aren't important, because they are, but only if the energy used to achieve them is significantly greater than the energy and investment expended to create them.

Developmental tasks are the longer term plans to create the dreams and desires that you build your success around. Without proper planning toward long-term desires, they'll sneak up on you and you won't be prepared to achieve them. Taking care of business every day to work the plans created for future tasks becomes significantly easier than rallying all of your energy to succeed in the moment.

What is relied on right now was created six months ago. It's easy to be motivated when the pressure is on, but can you be motivated when there's no pressure on to complete the task? That's the challenge.

As an athlete, your challenge is to balance the immediate needs with the developmental needs. This isn't easy, because the present demands will always carry more necessity and power, while the future desires will often be based on hope. And hope, as we've seen, is not an effective path to success because it implies a lack of awareness of the problem and no plan to overcome it. Future planning is often hope-based, but investing in developmental plans will overcome the immediate psychological pressures of the moment. By investing in the long term, the short term will become easier and easier over time.

3. **Training:**

For all athletes, Training is the key to staying ahead of the learning curve. It is about expanding the knowledge base and avoiding such risks to elite human performance as apathy, complacency, and mediocrity. Training isn't just important – it's mission critical. Everyone should identify activities that can help them train their brain on a daily basis – find articles, watch videos, or learn from others around you.

This is more than just heading to the gym and training the body. In fact, that would be a huge mistake. Training is about preparing the whole person to succeed, which also includes mental training.

It's important to find a way to expand your knowledge and skills. Does physical training prepare the mind? Absolutely — but only if the mind is engaged and ready to learn from it.

Training is like sharpening a knife. When a knife is dull, the amount of work it takes to sharpen the blade is directly proportional to the amount of surface area impacted. However, if you sharpen an already razor-sharp knife, it takes fewer strokes to get the blade to a perfect edge. Training is the same way. Too many athletes train in areas that aren't strengths and assume that the strengths will simply take care of themselves. That's a major mistake that even the best make.

Your strengths are your strengths for a reason. Too many assume that their strengths will continue to build and improve without their help, and thus no longer need to be focused on. Many elite athletes fall into this trap — they focus on their weaknesses rather than their strengths — but to succeed, you must continue to strengthen the things you do well. It's tempting, and seems to make common sense, to focus on the areas of your game that are giving you the most trouble.

Imagine that you're a basketball player. When the season's over, you review your season stats and notice that while you have a high three-point field goal percentage, your free-throw percentage is much lower than you expected it to be. The general coaching recommendation would be to spend hours and hours of extra time shooting from the free-throw line, and logic would seem to dictate that your free-throw percentage should rise accordingly. In fact, you should probably start shooting your free-throws as well as you shoot your three-pointers, with the same mental approach to make everything you shoot, right? Of course, because that's how athletes think.

The truth is, when an athlete diverts time and attention from one area of their training program to tend to a weakness, they rob valuable resources from a strength. The strength became a strength because it was worked on, built up, understood, and, often, fun. The athlete understands the ups and downs of their strength skills, and how doing more may not always show immediate improvements, but when it comes to their weaknesses, the same rationale rarely applies. A weakness is also a weakness for a reason.

I have a saying for my clients: "Those who use yesterday's results to determine today's preparation plan always live in a cycle of failure." Why? When the mindset is locked into responding to consistent weaknesses and failures, that becomes the goal. Every day, we live with failures and frustrations, but we also live with successes and growth. If we focus just on fixing the failures, we'll only see failure as important. Training must be bigger than that.

Training is about improving yourself physically and mentally. If it's designed primarily to improve your strengths, your strengths will continue to improve. You can always grow. You do need to work on your weaknesses, too, just not at the expense of your strengths. Making the psychological commitment to training daily emphasizes the mindset of development, growth, and continuous improvement. It's not about holding on to what you have, but growing your ability and competitive skillset.

4. Execution:

What separates great teams and athletes is their ability to execute under pressure, when it matters the most. If you're not preparing to execute, you'll miss the opportunity. Execution should be done on a daily basis and as a daily pursuit. How and what you are executing can differ from day to day, but you have to get in the frame of mind to challenge and work each and every day.

We can plan all day long, but there comes a point as athletes when it's time to get off our rear end and go do what we've been training to do. The motivation to compete and the will to filter through the different demands, distractions, and fears is what separates those who "want to" and those who "simply do." It's more than wanting to do something that creates great players.

There are no shortcuts. Watching the world's best is seductive because they make everything look so easy, but you don't see all the work they do when no one is watching, the hundreds of hours they spent climbing the ladder of success and the days and nights of doubts that stood in the way of their vision.

Your ability to execute on a daily basis, consistent with the plan and structure of your desires, is what differentiates success from mediocrity. Being average is great if you define average as being good enough. Average is desirable if you want a spot on the team or just want playing time. Great athletes, however, define average as a stop along the way to success. Daily execution of your plan takes discipline, commitment, and effort, factors with which those who accept average as their goal often struggle. Execute daily with consistency and the results will come much easier.

5. Review and Reflection:

This is the step that gets ignored the most. Despite all the things you may do on a daily basis, if you don't review and reflect on your experiences and lessons by journaling and/or meditating, you won't progress. Get a notebook and record everything you learned and the challenges you faced that day, and do it every day. You'll be amazed at the progress you make. Without it, all you have is the emotion of the day to determine progress, and emotion will lie to you every time.

Over the years, I've found that my most successful athletes journal their results. Men and women, young and old. The consistent factor is the psychological investment in journaling at the end of every practice and game.

Journaling provides so many psychological benefits and contributes so much to your education that it's necessary for growth. Remember, learning is the key to all performance and life development – if you fail to learn, you'll just repeat the same patterns. Without capturing your thoughts, emotions, and behaviors, you'll be robbing yourself of valuable learning opportunities.

The most beneficial aspect of journaling is the ability to track progress over time. At the end of each day or competitive/training activity, recording your experience will effectively capture the progress or difficulties of the day. By doing this, you are recording the quantitative and qualitative measures of your progress. For instance, if you felt that you struggled to cut additional time off of your race time during your last practice, simply recording the relevant times will provide a benchmark that you can use to measure your progress from the same time a year ago. It may be better, the same, or actually worse, but without measurements and an analytical comparison, the only evaluation tool you'll have is emotion. And emotion is a terrible evaluation tool.

When emotion is the main vehicle for analysis, progress is stunted. When emotions, particularly negative emotions, become elevated, the usual desire is to simply fix the problems, a strategy that, if you remember, causes you to abandon the plan and start over. This endless cycle of starting, stopping, and finding a new plan will spin you in circles, and you'll exhaust yourself.

Measuring progress is important in every facet of life. It doesn't matter how you record progress, as long as you take time every night to do it. Take time to review past entries and measure your improvements and areas for improvement.

Journaling also provides a valuable way to both release and analyze frustration and tension. When I first started to work with elite athletes, I wanted them to call me when they struggled. I felt that their ability to mentally process the game and have a resource to which they could vent would be beneficial. Unfortunately, instead of cognitively processing the ins and outs of the game, I found that I had to relive the game in its entirety. The players often wanted to go over things play by play – they were more interested in retelling the story than in processing the material.

As a result, I changed the process into more formal journaling. Using this process for journal entries was fantastic for my elite players, and it may also work for you. After every game (you can do this in practice, too), write down the three things that you did well in the game, three things that you struggled with, and three ways that you plan to invest in your improvement moving forward.

When reviewing the three positives from the day, be descriptive and thorough. Far too often, the positives get minimized, usually because athletes want to get after the negative aspects, even though the positives are the building blocks of your game. Learning to acknowledge your strengths helps build your self-image and your beliefs. Further, today's strengths may be areas that need improvement in the future, so documenting the period when you're doing well will provide you with a valuable progress check. There's nothing dangerous about knowing, believing, and trusting your strengths – nothing!

After recording the positives, list three things that you struggled with during the day. Once again, be careful to not make broad assumptions or categorizations of the negatives. The difficult aspects of your game were probably not as bad as you emotionally believe they were. And even if they were, the good news is that the terrible experience is over. The only way to process it is to journal it and let it go. Learn and then move on.

When reviewing the aspects of the day that didn't go as planned, there are essentially five ways to categorize the outcomes. By analyzing them this way, you increase your ability to process the information and move forward:

1. *Bad Preparation:*

   Preparation is the work you do to put yourself in the best position possible to succeed in your training. Sometimes, due to choices or external factors beyond your control, you're not adequately prepared for the competition. It happens to every athlete and team. If the greatest contributor to your struggle was a lack of preparation, use that disappointment as the discipline to get back into the proper preparation program. And there's no reason to beat yourself up about the lack of preparation – instead, use your angst to pay closer attention to your preparation details in the future.

2. _Bad Strategy:_

This is often overlooked and may be misunderstood for bad preparation, and in fact, preparation may be a contributor if the struggle is due to an ineffective strategy. Planning the in-game strategy is very important for many team sports, particularly when the strategy is designed to maximize your own strengths and take advantage of your opponent's weaknesses. Unfortunately, the chosen strategy is sometimes not effective. It happens. The effort may have been well intentioned, but it just didn't work. Your opponent may have had a better strategy, or you may have over-thought your own strategy, which led to even greater difficulty. I find that younger teams and coaches often overthink their strategy, which often causes them to rely on weaknesses or untested strategies in competition, rather than trusting what they've done well in training. Remember, as Chad Metcalf – the Navy SEAL turned professional golfer – told me, people don't rise up to the challenge; they fall to the level of their training. Bad strategies often overlook this. To remedy it, trust what you do every single day in training and what you can successfully complete over 80 percent of the time under pressure.

3. _Bad Execution:_

In the performance world, you're not a robot. There's nothing you can do with 100 percent precision every single time. As the pressure and the intensity of competition increases, it gets harder and harder to perform with absolute precision. I work with an elite collegiate gymnastics squad, and those athletes are beyond inspiring. During warm-ups, they continually hit their routines with perfection, but the challenge comes when they're being judged under the bright lights. This team, however, understands that execution is never a given, but something that needs to be invested in, so they're prepared to execute with the utmost precision and capacity when it matters the most. But there will be small variations, so instead of looking at execution as an absolute "all or nothing," review it as a percentage of completion. If your execution was less than 80 percent, understand that it could have been an aberration or an aspect that could benefit from more training. Your preparation and strategy may have been ideal, but you might not have executed a skill that you normally do with great precision – it happens, so just move on. Even the greatest occasionally miss a shot.

4. *Bad Mental Focus:*

Sometimes you just had a mental letdown at the moment that mattered the most, or, for a team, at exactly the wrong part of the game. Mental focus is a dynamic skill and there are times, due to a variety of physiological, psychological, and environmental factors, that your mental focus is simply not as sharp as it is at other times. Whether it was due to a lack of sleep, a poor diet, or the pressure of moment resulting in loss aversion or a preventative mindset, mental focus can be adversely impacted. If, when reviewing a poor outcome, you determine that a less than optimal amount of mental focus contributed to the adverse result, it's important to figure out what contributed to the loss of focus. Remember, learning is the pathway to mastery, so being aware of the circumstances under which your mental energy was robbed by other factors will help bolster and improve your focus in the future. It may even lead you to find ways to improve your focus in highly distracting environments, for example, or when you're tired, hungry, or not feeling well. Enhancing focus is a skill that can be learned. If your focus was the main factor behind a poor outcome, be aware of it and work to improve it for the next opportunity.

5. _Bad Fortune:_

When I was pitching, there were times when I did everything right – but the ball took a bad bounce and got by the infielders. It wasn't their fault and there was nothing I could do – it was just part of the game. In every sport, there will be times when you've done everything to the best of your ability but have still been beaten by a better opponent or a random, fluke of a play. Personally, I think bad fortune in sports is evened out by good fortune, but that doesn't make the instances of bad fortune feel any better. But when you've done everything in your power to succeed and still haven't, it's important to ask yourself if you really need to change anything moving forward. Why change something that doesn't have to be changed? Why raise alarms on a great mindset, strategy, and execution plan? Shit happens, right? Accept the outcome and move on. The bad fortune may come in waves, and you find yourself stuck in a period in which everything is going against you, but changing what you're doing and abandoning the plan will only cause more disruption into the performance model. Resist the urge and challenge yourself to be committed and aggressive in the face of bad fortune. It may turn in your favor moving forward.

After understanding what contributed to the areas of struggle, record how you plan to improve going forward. If you have a solid plan and process in place, it should be consistent with that. If you notice that your recommendations are different from your plan, seeing it on paper may prevent you from abandoning your plan all together. It's okay to make adaptations for continuous improvement, because all great plans are adapted over time, but the physical act of writing down the plan moving forward can really be a powerful act.

Journaling allows you to see things from a different perspective, especially when you put it away and read it at a later date. Your psychological motivations and emotional state change over time, so reviewing your past performances in life and sport to see where you were at that time can be an extremely valuable way to gain deeper insight into where you are now. Whether you're studying past progress or building a plan for the future, taking time every day to reflect through journaling will be a valuable investment into your overall productivity and success.

Doing these five things every day won't guarantee success, but not doing them will only cause unnecessary clutter and frustration during the day. Performing at a high level requires absolute mental focus and clarity, which allows you to make effective decisions, influence positive outcomes, and overcome challenges. When the mind is cluttered with inefficiency, mental energy that's needed just to survive is robbed from the drive to succeed.

Developing a daily strategy and executing it with purpose will only lead to an increased probability of success. You can develop the mental strategy of a world champion, but if your actions are that of a continual runner-up, the amount of psychological and mental energy needed to overcome the hole that you've built in your own life will be tough to come by. As the stakes get higher and higher, it will simply become more and more difficult to succeed. Talent alone may separate you from your competitors, but learning to do the little important details every day will increase your odds of success.

20

Surround Yourself with Those Better Than You

When I started The MindSide Podcast, the goal was to highlight the greatness in the world possessed by those immediately around me. I didn't want to go just out and hire a speaker; I wanted to learn from those people in my immediate circle. You may not realize it, but there is greatness all around you. Everyone is someone that you can learn from. Thankfully, the MindSide Podcast has become a huge success, thanks primarily to guests with amazing perspectives on life and the willingness to share them.

Who do you surround yourself with? The people around you are usually there for a reason, and part of the challenge is understanding what that reason is.

There's a lot of evidence that athletes train and compete better in groups. That's one reason that the U.S. Olympic Committee brings its athletes together for group training. It's important to build a team around you, much like a professional team has a large coaching and support staff on its payroll.

As an athlete, the easy answer is to surround yourself with coaches who will train you while providing you with support and encouragement. In fact, I hear that all the time. Unfortunately, I also shudder when I hear that.

Several years ago, I was working with a college softball team. The coach was trying very hard to build a legacy program that reflected the championship culture in which she had played. I thought she was working very hard to build the confidence of her team and show them what it took to win at the highest level, but she seemed to be encountering resistance at every level.

The team asked me to hold and lead a players-only meeting. Those meetings are usually difficult, because they're often used to share the frustrations of the past rather than to build a plan for the future. This one was no different.

The players began by complaining that the coaches weren't positive or encouraging in their daily practices and competitions. One player stood up and told the group that during a recent at-bat against a top-ranked team, she had worked the count to two balls and a strike – a great hitter's count. On the 2-2 pitch, she fouled the ball straight back. For hitters, fouling a pitch this way is often considered to be sign that they're timing and seeing the ball very well. Great hitters will normally see this as a positive and try to build off that confidence.

This player, however, stated that when she looked into the dugout after the fouled-off pitch, her coach didn't react or give her any positive feedback. I asked her what she ended up doing in the at-bat, and she told me that she struck out on the next pitch. She was quick to say, however, that if the coach had cheered for her on the fouled-off pitch, she would have probably had a better at-bat. She also added that when she returned to the dugout, her coach didn't say anything to her then, either! What a travesty, in the player's mind.

When I asked the team what they thought about her experience, their feedback was supportive of the player. The overwhelming majority of the team saw the coach's lack of a cheerful and positive response as a sign of a difficult coaching environment. I dug a bit deeper with the players and asked them what kind of coaching they wanted. I wasn't shocked, but I was a bit disgusted by the response.

Without question, the players were looking for "positive reinforcement" from their coaches. They told me that when the coaches corrected their technique or their actions on or off the field they tended to be too negative, which caused the players to resist the coaching and stop listening. One example they gave me was an incident in which their coach asked one player, "Why do you continue to not shift into position in the outfield when I try to move you?" By this point, I was sick to my stomach.

Positive reinforcement, or rewarding an action so that it continues, is a powerful tool in coaching, but it doesn't usually last for very long. Negative reinforcement, contrary to popular opinion, isn't punishment, but rather, the act of removing something adverse when the desired action is completed. An example would be eliminating end-of-practice conditioning if the team focuses successfully for the entire two-hour practice. This will likely raise the focus of the team, because they want to avoid doing the post-practice conditioning. Punishment is introducing something adverse, painful, or uncomfortable as a way to stop a behavior or action from occurring. These players had come to enjoy positive reinforcement – after all, it's a very pleasurable thing – but they eventually came to see any lack of positive reinforcement, for any reason whatsoever, as punishment.

Players who only want positive reinforcement in their lives are trying to avoid success. There is a time and place for praise, rewards, and public displays of encouragement. The problem arises when this is the only form of coaching that's deemed effective. That's a trap.

People are in our lives for a reason. As players, you may not appreciate the style or intensity of your coach in the moment. In fact, you may finish your career with your coach or trainer and not have many positive things to say about them, but overtime, the realization of the constructive impact on your life will become evident. For every coach I had in my life, through sports and my professional psychology career, each served a different role that was important in that time in my life. If I had dismissed them because their approach or message was not what I was wanting at that time, I would have limited the growth over the extended period of time. My resistance would have limited my growth. Players and coaches must build a network of people around them who directly and indirectly make them better. You really need the five following people:

1. Competitors:

You want individuals around you who naturally engage the competitive nature of your mind and soul. That may be an intrasquad nemesis or a workout partner with whom you go toe-to-toe, but in any case, it's someone you really have to work hard against to beat. Competitive mindsets aren't innate, they have to be fostered, developed, and refined. The best way to do that is to work hard while competing against someone on a regular basis.

A valuable competitor is someone you can measure yourself against on a daily basis. As they raise the bar, you have to raise your level of execution, too. A great competitor is someone who relishes the opportunity to compete and who raises their own level of effort, execution, and commitment simply to beat you. When you're in that environment, both sides benefit.

How do competitors contribute to your success?

Being in an environment in which you're driven to compete with another forces you to break your Fishbowl and stretch your comfort zones. I see this happen first-hand with junior academies. When athletes start to become acclimated to the academy nature, the competition ramps up with every drill, intrasquad game, and round. Those who are more engaged in the competition simply pass those who can't handle the controlled nature of the competitive environment. Competitors feed off each other to improve.

The competitive environment benefits those who are competing against one another. If you look back at the history of sport, those intense rivalries have always raised the level of performance. In the 1980s, the National Basketball Association (NBA) benefited from a competitive rivalry between Earvin "Magic" Johnson of the Los Angeles Lakers and Larry Bird of the Boston Celtics. Every matchup was intensely played, with both players and their teams pushing each other to new levels. There is no doubt that both teams had their rivals in their crosshairs in every practice and offseason training program.

Competitors are healthy if they're understood properly. In every line of work, business, and sport, an identified rival can help provide needed motivation and intensity. Where the possible struggle of having a competitor may arise is when you abandon the plan and purpose of your own preparation simply to meet the demands of that one competitor and ignore the others who want to beat you. That distraction is common among collegiate and professional teams that have letdowns after rivalry games. To avoid that, use a competitor to push you through a low spot, but maintain a focus on your overall capability and capacity to compete.

2. Challengers:

This is different than a competitor – it's a coach or other athlete who can openly challenge your beliefs, training style, and mindsets. What I mean by "challenger" is that this is the person who can call your bullshit and to whom you have to be accountable.

A challenger is hard on you, pushing you and demanding more of you than you ever thought you were capable. A challenger is often someone who has a completely different point of view from yours. If you're politically liberal, meeting someone who's conservative can be beneficial – not so you have someone to yell and scream at, but so you have someone to share your individual perspectives with, which in turn will enhance the knowledge and depth of your own perspective. Our opinions in life and sport are often somewhat shallow, and only by challenging and being challenged by others do we better formulate the nature of our work.

Facing a challenger requires preparation and intense training. If you're a coach, a challenger would be another coach who sees the game completely differently. Sitting down and having an in-depth discussion about the intricate nature of an offense when you come from completely different perspectives can be difficult. Simple answers just don't cut it.

Several years ago, I was sitting in first class on a long transcontinental flight when a young millennial sat down next to me. He was dressed in designer blue jeans and flip-flops, and carried himself with confidence. As the plane reached cruising altitude, he started talking to me and asking me questions about what I did for a living and where I was going. I normally refrain from airplane conversations, but since we were waiting for our dinner, it was hard to avoid. I'm glad I didn't avoid the conversation. He told me that he had started a large database company in college and had sold the company in his junior year for a significant amount of money. While still in school, he worked in Congress and spent time with some great business leaders. Eventually he became bored and decided to start a new company, which was now a major international technology firm with offices around the world.

As we talked, he was open and honest about his management style, and I still use many of the lessons I learned that day. The most important thing was the importance of having one to three challengers in your close circle.

Corporate executives often place a challenger on the company's board to question all decisions. Problems arise, however, when the whole board becomes challengers, which can often happen when the company is struggling or the leader lacks confidence or vision. Good challengers, however, know when to provide feedback and when to challenge. Having a strong member of your team as a challenger can push you to focus on your own philosophy and to find material to support that philosophy. It's hard to put those people in your life, but they're critical for success.

The young businessman on the plane told me that he had a clear policy for his company and his board – a few are charged with challenging the direction of the business, while the rest are responsible for implementing the strategy to their fullest potential. Early in his career, he maintained an open e-mail address for suggestions and critiques of the company, but he ended up spending so much time responding to the e-mail suggestions from all levels of the company that he lost focus on the daily job of running the company. Those whose role is to challenge the company aren't expected to just be contrarian, but rather, to provide solutions in areas that need improvement. He told me that when he began to identify and trust the challengers in his life, his business reached all-time profit levels.

It can be hard to have challengers in your life, but without them, it's easy to fall back into the habits and safety of mediocrity. Educate the challengers as to why they're in your life, and demand their honesty and valued solutions. Only then will your game improve.

3. Critiquers:

The critiquer is different than a challenger for one primary reason: His or her job is to be critical of your approach, technique, and effort in significantly greater detail than a challenger. While a challenger is there to challenge each aspect of you from a new and different perspective, a critiquer's job is to look at how you do things and to review the intricate nature of your approach in great detail.

In the athletic world, a critiquer is usually a coach or support person who may have additional training in the technical or strategic aspect of your game. Many athletes resist as soon as a coach starts to critique their technique or provide directed feedback. In fact, resistance is always the first response to feedback – *always*. It doesn't matter who you are or how enlightened you may be – resistance is a natural response to directed, constructive feedback. But great athletes and leaders move past this resistance so that they can evaluate the information and, more importantly, the person providing that feedback. If that person is valued, the information will probably have greater impact. Insecure athletes or those who are deep in the fog of the Learning Cycle may simply listen to anyone with feedback and abandon their plan for the next quick fix. Having appointed and valued critiquers in your life can overcome this challenge.

There are many ways that critiquers can effectively provide constructive feedback, such as through statistical review, video review, or verbal descriptive recollection. Video review can be very instructive for an athlete. In today's athletic culture, they're relied on more and more to help identify weaknesses and to show what's needed to improve.

Several years ago, I was working with an elite college basketball program and had to intervene on a series of problems the coaching staff was having with the team. Resistance from the players was hindering the role of video review and analysis. As the coaching staff's critiquer was reviewing game film – a common practice after both wins and losses – he began to notice that certain players were laughing throughout the video review. The coach asked me after one particular video session how to handle the disruptive players, and we explored the motivations of the offenders.

What we noticed was surprising. When the review was focused on the troubles of other players, these two or three players would make small jokes and engage in some lighthearted razzing of their teammates. If a teammate had been dunked on, for example, these players would ramp up the jokes for a few minutes, just to make sure that the player in question knew not only that he had embarrassed himself in the game, but that he was now also being shamed by his peers, as well. It was often very easy for the coaching staff and support team to get caught up in the razzing, too, particularly when the players were usually *SportsCenter* worthy.

The tone and tenor changed, however, when the players who were in charge of the public ridicule were themselves the focus of the review session, and before long a shaming battle between players had erupted. The problem was that with each lighthearted shame attempt, the players missed a good lesson on how to improve. The better players, not surprisingly, didn't enjoy being the focus of the corrective film sessions, and they managed to eventually get the whole room in an uproar. The more the coach would try to get the film review focused on critical review and improvement, the more the players would resist and act out.

The correction wasn't that hard, but it required an educational session from the head coach. Prior to the next review session, the coach and I stood in front of the team and explained the role of the film session, the importance of critical analysis, and why it was so hard to sit and listen to difficult feedback. We made it clear that not only was a critiquer there to make them better, it was evidence of how much the staff really cared for each player. After all those who are unwilling to share important and constructive feedback because they're concerned about how it might be received are often more concerned about themselves than about helping others.

From that meeting forward, film sessions were dramatically different. Coach would quickly enlist teammates to share what they saw in each video and ask for constructive teammate input, particularly from older players. That helped create a culture of continuous improvement to which the older players responded, eventually leading the team to the NCAA tournament.

Receiving constructive feedback can help pinpoint a player's insecurities. Of course, when people are presented with new information that differs from their current perspective, they have a natural tendency to resist. It's a normal human reaction to put up defenses when faced with critical feedback, because it often attacks our self-image and self-confidence.

To find a critiquer, you must first be willing to listen to the feedback. It's hard to have your heart and soul exposed for others to critique, and understandably difficult to let down your defenses. Nevertheless, accepting and listening to feedback is critical for success.

Second, you should try to find a critiquer who has more knowledge about your particular area of expertise than you do. It can be a mentor or someone who's walked in the same shoes in the past, but make sure you avoid people who have a limited perspective. It'll only hurt you in the long run.

Finally, tell them clearly what you're trying to improve and what their role should be in this improvement. Trust me — giving someone feedback is just as difficult as receiving it. Think about the last time you were with a friend and they had a booger hanging from their nose – it's hard to point something like that out without potentially hurting their feelings or embarrassing them. Of course, the problem is that saying nothing will probably make things worse, so make sure to establish an environment in which feedback is heard and accepted by you.

A critiquer is probably the most important person you can find for your own development. Take the time to find that person and seek out their expertise. Listen and thank them for their investment in your future. It's definitely worth it.

4. Confidence Builders:

Developing an elite mindset and a heightened performance repertoire is not always about being critiqued and challenged. Praise can often feel good, especially during difficult times. Amazingly enough, however praise can also be hard for some people to handle.

Work on surrounding yourself with people who help build your confidence. Ultimately, no one can really build your confidence but you, but having supportive people around you who are willing to give you a little pat on the back for your successes can be beneficial. On every successful coaching staff, there is usually one coach who's easy for the players to talk to and who serves as a positive resource. The reason for this is simple: It helps build a positive buffer from the challenges of competition, coaching, and the pursuit of greatness.

This is a great role for parents, especially when their children progress past them in coaching or technical competence. Parents can serve such a positive influence over their athletic children, but it can also be a high-risk environment unless it's managed successfully. In fact, a poorly managed parent-athlete relationship can be devastating to the athlete's long-term success.

Surround Yourself with Those Better Than You

When my oldest daughter was playing junior and high school golf, I fell into the same dangerous waters in which so many parents find themselves. My daughter was a good golfer, but she was very cognizant of my actions while I was watching. As I walked and followed her group, I often stood with my arms crossed, occasionally biting my fingernails, and I was apparently unaware of the facial expressions I was making behind my sunglasses. On more than one occasion, my daughter would look over to me and ask what was wrong. Nothing was, but it was obvious that I wasn't helping her or being a supportive confidence builder.

I later learned that while it was comfortable to stand with my arms crossed, my body language made it look to my daughter as though I was constantly angry or disappointed. In fact, nothing could have been further from the truth. After we had a discussion one night, she told me how I made her feel while she was playing, and I felt terrible. From that point on, I started to chew on sunflower seeds at her matches instead of biting my fingernails, and I also started listening to music on my earphones, which actually changed my facial expressions. The results were instantaneous. She played fantastically well for the rest of her senior year.

Confidence builders and parents play a major role in a young athlete's success. It's a great responsibility to remain positive and supportive even when the player has a bad day, so make sure you choose confidence builders who can temper their own emotions and put yours first. It's a tough job.

Parents and confidence builders should heed the following advice when serving in this role:

1. Don't try to provide any technical or corrective feedback for three hours after the event. It's easy to see the necessary corrections when you're not playing, but right after a game or match, most players are still highly emotional and engaged in the competitive mindset. They probably won't hear the message, but they probably will react to your attempt to

coach them. Instead, ask them where they want to eat after the game. You'll be shocked at how differently they respond.

2. Tell them how much you enjoy watching them compete and how proud you are of their effort. If they struggled in that game, try to find something that they can control and highlight that as a positive. Things such as a "sticking to it," effort, and hustle are great examples.

3. Avoid using excuses for the outcome. Talking about an umpire's questionable call, a bad coaching decision, or the failure of a teammate isn't an effective way to smooth over a mediocre performance. Furthermore, if your player has a good day, be gracious and supportive of the other players. Don't "peacock" or highlight the great play to other parents and families. Accept any praise, but understand that for every good day, there's a tough day in the investment bank that has helped make that day possible.

4. Finally, ask your player what they thought of their own performance. Too often, we project our own feelings and expectations onto the player, when in fact, he or she may be pleased with how they competed.

Confidence builders can also be those with whom you compete daily and have an advantage over. It's hard to compete against and defeat those who have nothing to lose. If they're used to getting beat, you still run a risk of failing to successfully stay focused on the task at hand.

5. Colleagues:

Colleagues are the final piece of your support network. These are the people who share the same experiences with you. They've been there and walked the same walk. But even though they have similar experiences, colleagues may have different perspectives that can help you.

Most great organizations and teams try to pair younger athletes with more senior mentors for exactly this reason. Colleagues understand, first hand, the challenges you face, and they can help you avert some of the mistakes that they made.

You can often share first-hand experiences with colleagues and ask them questions. The person could be someone who was drafted in the same round as you were, someone who has recently gone through a contract negotiation, or someone who recently completed the college recruiting process. Their knowledge will be invaluable if you're willing to listen and learn.

Colleagues can often serve as effective mentors, too. Identifying those individuals in your life who can support you from a different psychological level – such as a colleague who's invested in your good and bad experiences – will facilitate a healthy growth platform. Finding someone who can be a mentor and a colleague, however, can be difficult.

Early in my career, I tried to reach out to business leaders from different industries and learn as much as I could from them. I'd offer to take them to lunch or meet at a local coffee shop, and I'd sit and ask them questions about learning, business, and organizational growth. I was completely transparent with them about the reason for the invitation, but I desperately wanted to learn from those who had walked similar paths before me.

What I took from those meetings was that by listening to the valuable lessons that those mentors had to offer, I could provide better perspectives into what I was about to experience or painful lessons from my past. Many of the lessons I learned in sports, business, and life are associated with painful experiences. But as happens when you're trying to overcome an illness, if you have perspective from an expert about how your recovery is likely to progress, it makes the struggle somewhat easier.

One such colleague for me was a gentleman who played baseball at LSU several years before me. He was a local player like me, and after his playing days were over, he stayed around the program.

He was also busy building a financial services organization and made frequent presentations to the baseball team on the topic of financial stewardship. I got to know Pete Bush on a number of different levels, but after I was finished playing, he remained a significant colleague for me, even though he may not realize it to this day. When I need some professional advice or suggestions about things that he's gone through in his life, I reach out to him. He always responds, and I greatly value our time together. The lessons that I've learned from him have been invaluable.

When I was in graduate school and my wife was pregnant with our first child, I ran into Pete at a local restaurant. He was running in from his office and grabbing something from the takeout window, but he saw me eating alone and walked over for a brief chat. Thanks to the pleasantries of a random meeting in a busy restaurant, he provided me with some insight into his life that I never forgot. He was going through a divorce, a fact that I didn't know at that time, and he simply said "Your work isn't so important that you can't be home with your family for dinners and on weekends."

It was a powerful statement, and one that I had heard many times. My mother and father always tried to be home for dinner, and if we couldn't manage that, we'd try to meet somewhere for a quick meal together before going our separate ways. Pete knew that I was pushing to succeed and that my wife and I were expecting our first child. I've never forgotten that piece of advice, and when I'm sitting in the office working and dinner is approaching, I think back to that conversation in the restaurant. It usually makes me stop what I'm doing and head home to my family.

A mentor or colleague doesn't have to wear a name tag or even know that you see them as filling such a role. It definitely helps deepen the relationship, but whether they know or not, I encourage you to develop colleagues and mentors in your life. It will pay significant dividends.

Surround Yourself with Those Better Than You

Remember, one of the drives of life is social acceptance, but that can cloud the impact that the five people in your life have on you. Look beyond your immediate needs and understand the developmental impact that these people can have on your sport and life. Through their guidance, mentoring, and coaching, your success can be pushed to new levels. As an athlete, try to surround yourself only with those who will make you better. There is no sense in wasting time on people who simply drain your energy.

If you're questioning the value of a person in your life, ask yourself if they fall into one of the five categories. In sport, you're dealing with hundredths of seconds between first and second place. If they're not helping you gain an advantage, they're merely causing you to perform below your abilities.

21

Declaring Your Manifesto

We all live behind a mask. Every day, you work hard to project yourself in a manner consistent with how you want to be seen by the world, but that's rarely how you truly see yourself. The mask is powerful.

During my freshman season at LSU, we had a talented center fielder who had transferred in from a junior college. Danny Zahl was a powerful player – fast, great hitter, and a major-league arm. He was brash, confident, aggressive on the field, and a huge factor in our early-season success.

Unfortunately, Zahl never finished the season. One night, a bunch of my teammates were hanging out in my apartment when Zahl knocked on the door. He had been suspended for a violation of team rules, having failed too many drug tests for smoking marijuana. He said he was taking full responsibility, and that even though the tests suggested that he had more of a problem than he really did, he was choosing to go into treatment and would miss the rest of the season. It was the first time I had ever been around a situation like that – it was like losing a brother, and we weren't even that close. In fact, I was scared to death of him.

The team moved on quickly. Armando Rios immediately took over in center field and performed very well. Rios was from Puerto Rico, and he immediately became a fan favorite thanks to his outgoing, vivacious personality. Rios was one of my roommates, and he simply loved the spotlight. No stage was too big – not even national television and the national championship game.

During the 1991 National Championship game against Wichita State, a perennial college baseball power in the 1980s and '90s, Rios took over. He was responsible for several runs, made a number of great plays, and homered in the late innings to give LSU the lead, which it wouldn't relinquish. After the final out, as the rest of the team was piling up in the middle of the infield, Rios was doing a roundoff back handspring in front of the live network television audience. Zahl, meanwhile, watched the game from the day room in his inpatient rehabilitation center, later admitting that he was experiencing a wide range of emotions, including pride, sadness, and jealousy.

I lost track of Zahl after the season. He transferred out and only stayed in touch with a few of our teammates. He didn't attend the White House ceremony where President George H.W. Bush and baseball legends and Hall of Famers Ted Williams and Joe DiMaggio honored our national championship team. In fact, most of us wouldn't see or hear from him again for another twenty years.

Thanks to the power of social media, it soon became clear why Zahl had basically disappeared after college. When he showed up at our twentieth-anniversary reunion, he was noticeably different. The striking good looks had changed. His face was different. It wasn't until that day that I learned of Danny Zahl's struggle and the depths to which the once-promising college baseball player had fallen.

He told the team that he'd been to hell and back over the previous two decades, but that he was walking a powerfully healing path now. For ten or fifteen years after our national championship season, Zahl had spiraled out of control into drugs and alcohol. After a toxic relationship ended, he decided to kill himself. He placed a shotgun under his chin, yelled, and pulled the trigger.

Amazingly, the physical act of yelling saved his life. It moved his head back slightly, and while the gun's discharge destroyed his jaw and face, it spared his brain.

Zahl spent months in intensive care, and has now had more than forty-five surgeries to repair his jaw, eyesight, and facial structures. Obviously, he's lucky he's alive. But the truth is, we're all lucky he's alive. His story can teach every one of us a valuable lesson.

After reconnecting with Zahl, I asked him to come and share his story with my teams and young athletes. It took him about five years to take the plunge, but I remained patient. His story was important, but his health was more important.

When Zahl came in, he sat in front of a large team and shared his story and testimony. Throughout his college career and early adulthood, he hid from the truth and used drugs to escape from the pain of honesty. It was easier to flood life with the relief that his drug of choice gave him than it was to look in the mirror. He was lying to himself, and although he enjoyed a pretty fair amount of success in the business world both before and after the shooting, was lying to every person in his life.

After we spent several days together, Zahl's underlying issue became obvious to me. He had been living his life behind a mask, hiding from the pain, depression, and anxiety from which he suffered every day. His facial reconstruction had made the physical part of that mask permanent, but not the emotional and self-perception parts. Those were different.

When Zahl finally took off the perception mask, he became vulnerable at a level that he had never experienced before in his life. He'd been avoiding life's What Ifs for a very, very long time, desperate to protect himself from the person he feared he was. Instead of embracing the real Danny Zahl, he did what so many of us do – he projected himself as he wanted the world to see him, instead of who he really was.

Zahl was forced to understand struggle at a level that would have been unthinkable to him earlier in life. He could no longer hide behind excuses or transfer the blame. By telling his story, he forced himself to get out of his comfort zone and break the constraints of his fishbowl, which was clouded and not a healthy place for him to live. This act seemed natural for me and the rest of our former teammates, but for Danny Zahl, who was living in a scary world, it required deep conviction and trust.

How would he be judged if he messed up? How would he feel about himself if this new way of life didn't produce the results he was desperate to achieve but terrified to admit to himself? How would he overcome the doubts that clouded his fishbowl and the belief in his ability to survive, when he had never really fully lived before?

By declaring his Manifesto, Zahl was forced to state how he was going to live his life moving forward. It would be scary, it would be painful, but he was going to take off the mask and do it. He would no longer stand behind fear, apathy, and the status quo. He told me that he had lives to change. By sharing his story, he wanted other athletes, students, and parents to know that pain is simply a signal that something needs to be addressed. Not the symptom – the core.

I stay in touch with Danny on a regular basis. He's trying to live his Manifesto on a daily basis. It hasn't been easy, but he's been authentic to himself. He's healed his relationships and finally leveled with his family. Most importantly, he's finally leveled with the man in the mirror. He's begun speaking to groups, and his first-ever public discussion about his struggles took place on The MindSide Podcast. His second such talk took place in front of 150 members of a national championship organization. It went flawlessly, primarily because it was authentic and straight from the heart.

Once you tap into your Manifesto, life flows. It's much more rewarding to stand exposed without the mask you've hidden behind for your whole life than to project a fake self, hiding your fears and your desires and just living to survive.

Taking the mask off is your choice. No one else can do it for you. No one can believe in you more than you believe in yourself. You won't get an invitation and a safe place to do it. Life isn't easy. Sports aren't easy. But they are your life and your experience.

It's important to understand that I'm not advocating that you recklessly break with everything you've ever known to gain your freedom. I am advocating that you listen to your heart and declare how *you* want to see the world from your own mental perspective. I'm telling you – yelling at you, screaming at the top of my lungs at you – to take off the mask that you've been hiding behind and declare how you plan to take on the world.

No team or player succeeds without a game plan that has been built on a known underlying philosophy. It starts everything for the mental perspective, and that starts with your Manifesto. If you're not capable or strong enough to declare it in front of your peers – not necessarily by what you say but by how you act – then it's not important enough for you yet. But more likely, it's not clear to you yet, either.

To fully determine your Manifesto, you need to free yourself of the protection and safety nets on which you've relied for so long. I was scared to death to succeed and to have my teammates rely on me, but deep down I was terrified that I wouldn't continue to succeed after my previous success. To overcome that, I had to forcibly define what I wanted more than anything else, and I had to be willing to deal with failure. By assuring myself that I was okay with failing, I was free to invest everything I had in succeeding.

As an athlete, coach, parent, or student, living according to your Manifesto is so much more rewarding than not being true to it. A competitor who only does enough to get by will never realize his or her potential or talent. A coach who coaches to not lose and hopes to win by default creates such stress on a team that they're burned by the heat of failure. At the end of the day, would you rather fully invest and fail, or not fully realize your potential?

Your call to action takes understanding and insight. I challenge you to take the time to learn more about yourself. Start by looking in the mirror and asking yourself these questions:

1. If I couldn't fail, how would I take on life?
2. How does fear or apathy impact me?
3. If I continue on the path I'm on now, will I be satisfied or disappointed?
4. What aspects, attributes, and resources do I have that can help me succeed?
5. When I fail to live up to expectations, why have I failed? What constants always seem to pop up?
6. If I declare how I want to see and interact with the world, what could I really lose?
7. What do I really want?

Declaring your Manifesto won't produce immediate results. If you're doing this for immediate satisfaction or relief, it's not a Manifesto – it's a Band-Aid. Living according to your Manifesto is a long-term process and approach. There will be benefits and there will be challenges. Every experience is a learning experience, and you now know how hard learning is and the emotional pain, frustration, and confusion that come with it.

When you walk into the weight room at the gym, you start with the proper movements and repetitions before adding more weight. It's about building up your capability to perform, and then, over time, developing the capacity to succeed in the challenge. The Manifesto is no different.

Your Manifesto is to be declared and grown through challenges and learning opportunities in sport and life. With the intent and purpose of your Manifesto, every game you play is an experience to be learned from. That's the importance of having a structured review plan every single day and after every competition. Without it, you'll be very disappointed. The motivation of many is to fix the problems in their competitive life, but if you're not learning, and you're falling prey to that motivation, you're simply ignoring the drive for accomplishment and mastery.

Believing that you have the ability to persevere and grow is living your Manifesto fully. But you can't grow what you don't declare. Growth is hard. Sports are hard. Life is hard. Competition and success are even harder.

Developing and competing with your Manifesto opens you up to all sorts of outcomes. Success and failure are simply categories, not definitions of value. For every success, there is the need to raise the bar. For every failure, there is the desire to overcome. But in the moment, both have benefits.

Living according to your Manifesto will be freeing. Competing from your Manifesto is what you train yourself for with every early morning workout, every grueling practice, and every challenging battle. There are many, many talented players competing to get to the top of the mountain, but only those who fully believe in themselves, who know who and what they are at a deep level, and who are willing to fail so that they can succeed will continually stand on top of the mountain.

The Manifesto is your declaration of excellence. From there, the pathway and details of your success are simply challenges that you'll need to tackle on a daily basis. Those who get bored, lose. Those who take the easy way out, lose. Those who quit on themselves, fail.

I'm not talking about one game. Luck always happens, but over time, the best of the best do the things that others simply don't have the guts to do. They make sacrifices in their life, they face their own fears and doubts when they look in the mirror, and most importantly, they live according to their Manifesto.

22

What Now? Break Free and Own Your Game and Life

When I share the importance of adopting a manifesto and adhering to its intent, athletes are immediately energized and ready to get moving. The passion and energy for the immediate change is empowering and their minds shift to all the different facets of their lives that they can change to create the future that they want. Unfortunately, that passion does not last long. When the motivation of the moment is not bolstered by a consistent approach, it will fade away.

Throughout my career, I have been fortunate to hear presentations given by national leaders, astronauts, Grammy-winning musicians, and best-selling authors on motivation and personal empowerment. At each presentation, I always take detailed notes and leave with enthusiasm ready to take on the world.

In one such presentation, a photographer delivered a message I will never forget. His name is Dewitt Jones and his talk was one of quiet determination of purpose and leadership that truly inspired immediate change, consistent with living through a manifesto. Jones is one of the nation's leading photographers, having captured the beauty and crisis of the world for *National Geographic* for many years. His attention to detail and ability to look beyond the standard approach of photography has differentiated his approach from his contemporaries.

During his 90-minute keynote presentation, there was not a sound from the audience. Throughout his talk, he bounced back and forth from the catalog of award-winning photography on the projection screen and his lessons from life. His message was clear: learn to see life differently because shifting your perspective changes everything.

To emphasize this point, Jones showed a picture of a beautiful flower on the side of a mountain. In this picture, he highlighted the contrast of the dark granite on the side of the mountain, the rich blue colors of the sky in the background, and rich yellow petals of the flower. The contrast was powerful and was reflective of his ability as a photographer to draw on the contrasts to capture the beauty of the planet. But he was not done.

On the next slide was a picture of the same flower, but from a completely different perspective. The breathtaking beauty of the first picture was not enough for Jones; he demanded more. He recounted how as he stood on that mountain, he challenged himself to see the flower from a different perspective. It was a conscious choice directly influenced by the beauty of the environment but fueled by his passion to see the world from a different angle in every assignment he was given.

In the new picture, the flower was now in the top of the frame, with the deep, rich blue sky resting behind each petal, drenched in the glory of the sun's rays flowing between the petals like running water. By seeing the flower from down on the ground, resting on the painfully sharp granite rocks of the mountain, he captured a Pulitzer Prize winning photograph. Same flower, different perspective, award-winning.

In every field and competitive environment, there is a battle that is waged between the status quo and innovation. The status quo is governed by the desire to remain comfortable with the predictable, safe approach. Innovation requires discomfort and a hunger to experience new frontiers of your own ability. The individual pieces of this battle are between belief and doubt, desire and protection, and hope and fear. It is the battle of growth and stagnation. The greatest challenge is not with the competition or the world, but within you – a battle that is waged every single day.

As you take this mentality of purpose and intent forward, consider the value of the learning that will take place. Just like the award-winning photographer, Jones, learned the value of seeing the world from a different perspective, each experience in your life serves as a playground for learning and growth. The most important skill that you can embody is being open to the learning of life.

There will be days that you feel like you are going backwards, flushing away all the positive growth that you have experienced up to that moment. Those traps and struggles are not predictive in their presence, but rather inspiring to re-engage to the importance of resiliency and purpose of the journey.

There will be great days as well. Through the good and the bad, what will not change is your mindset and the inherent nature of you. When you invest in developing and expanding your mindset, one that is built on having purpose, intent, and desire, it shifts away from the traps and ruts of life and sport. Having a mindset that bets on you and your strengths inspires every action to invest in your ability and capacity to perform in the moment.

Every great athlete I have ever worked with plays from a strong, driven mindset, one of desire and purpose. They truly embody the manifesto approach. Sure – they suffer from periods of doubts and insecurity, distractions and exhaustion, but they believe in themselves more than others. It is that self-belief in the ability and their mindset that drives them to continual success. It becomes an undeniable force.

For you to succeed in implementing and living through your manifesto, it is critical that you continue to invest in your development and growth through each experience in your sport and life. It will be easy to see the challenges of the moment as invitations to abandon that approach and start over, but learn from the lessons of this book to stay the course, adapt and overcome. With each experience, positive and negative, you are closer to your desires.

So, as *The MindSide Manifesto* is coming to an end as a book but shifting to a call-to-action in your competitive environment, I want to leave you with a few tips to get started and stay the course.

1. **Take the time to learn what you truly want.** It has to come from you. If it is for someone else, it will not happen. For those who are successful, the personal desire drives success. Be clear with what you want and be descriptive. If you want to be All-District in your sport, admit that to yourself and declare it. Too often I have athletes who will describe everything but what they truly want. It is not up to others to judge what you want or if it

is possible, all that matters is that you are honest with yourself about what you truly want.

2. **Establish what your philosophy is in life.** For any new business that is getting started, it is important that they define what type of business they want to conduct, who their target market is, and how they will run their business. For restaurants, they have to declare what type of cuisine, if it is fast food, family casual, or fancy so they can market and advertise to recruit the clientele to match their presentation. They do not just open their doors and cook food made-to-order with a hodge-podge of decorations. You must do the same thing. For me, I made the decision that I was more comfortable as a relief pitcher in baseball. I was happy to be a starter, but I liked relief better. I did the same thing in my career path, I am fully comfortable as a clinical psychologist and honestly, I am pretty good at providing clinical services, but I enjoy at a much deeper level working with athletes so I decided to only do sports and performance psychology. When I started The MindSide, I developed my philosophy and that has influenced every aspect of my professional life since. I would recommend taking the time to write down the factors of your mental game that fits into your philosophy. Do you like to play and compete with adrenaline or peace of mind? Do you like to prepare with a strong physical purpose or do you like to leave practice with energy? Explore the nature of your game and identify your overall philosophy to competition.

3. **Work through your strengths.** Too many, as has been discussed in this book, get caught up in fixing their weaknesses instead of working through and consistently improving their strengths. Know your strengths and work through them every day in your game.

4. **Understand what you are willing to sacrifice to be successful.** For many athletes, girlfriends/boyfriends, friends, and families may inadvertently cause stress and anxiety for the athlete because they do not understand the time commitments

necessary to reach your goals. Unfortunately, the athlete's loved ones mean well, but may distract the athlete from their training or question why the athlete needs to take extra time in the weight room or gym to improve, since practice is over. But for the elite athletes, practice is just the starting point. Great athletes find time outside of practice and competition to refine their craft. You must be willing to make those sacrifices and educate your loved ones on what you need to do to reach your goals.

5.   Once you decide what you want, what your underlying philosophy is, and how to build through your strengths and understanding what needs to be sacrificed, all that is left is to **be unrelenting in your pursuit of your goals**. Your mindset will fuel your actions if you trust the process and have patience with the journey. Understand that your resiliency and determination is formed from your underlying self-belief, so believe in you and your Manifesto.

It all begins in the mind. There is nothing magical about fighting for your desires and being unrelenting to achieve it. The only way that you are going to see the power of your ability to create the success on the field and in life that you desire is breaking free from the fears, doubts, and insecurities that you have now. You did not pick up this book because you wanted to learn how to keep doing what you are doing right now. If you only learned one thing is this book, I want it to be that your mindset is everything. Believe it in so strongly that it becomes your Manifesto.

If you establish your Manifesto and invest in living it every single day, the successes and failures of life will transform into growth accelerators. I have never met a successful person who lacked a belief in their ability to succeed and you will not be the first. It is time to shift your mindset to one of urgency, purpose, and desire. It is time to Live Your Manifesto.

Post-Script

I want to thank you for taking the time to read about a perspective that is so important in my life. This book was more than a project for me. It became a reflective journey into the successes and failures of my own life. That is why the book has a strong autobiographical perspective.

Each and every one of you embodies the power to create what you want to achieve in your life. It may not result in what you originally envisioned at the outset of the journey, but in the end, it will be exactly what you needed to achieve.

While at LSU, Coach Bertman used numerous different motivational quotes to educate his teams. While we would laugh and snicker when he would share them, each player to this day can recite them verbatim. It is not about knowing the words for those who wore the Purple and Gold on the baseball diamond, it is about knowing the meaning behind the words. Despite passing them off as funny, each player took in the words to their own philosophy of life. As such, I am going to leave you with two quotes that I hold on to and apply every single day. Thank you for allowing me to share my story and share the importance of The Manifesto. Go attack life!

"If it is to be, it is up to me."

– William H. Johnson (1901-1970)
World-renown African-American painter.

"Whatever you vividly imagine, ardently desire, sincerely believe, and enthusiastically act upon…must inevitably come to pass!"

– Paul J. Meyer (1928-2009)
Founder of Success Motivation Institute, one of the original and most successful motivational speakers in the United States.

Acknowledgements

Writing a book is not a singular process. It is the reflection of years of work and countless hours of writing, editing, and revisions. In the case of this book, it is much greater than that. It is a reflection of my life and all those who have positively influenced it.

Thank you to David DeNunzio of Golf Magazine for the guidance and support, and to Gary Perkinson for the professional editing and copy review. Thank you to Hunter Crawford for the design, inside and out. And thank you to the team at The MindSide, Donnette Hulsey and Meighan Julbert, for the support to write this book. Thank you to Lee Feinswog for helping me see the power that I had within me the whole time.

From a professional perspective, I want to personally thank those who helped train me as a psychologist. To Dr. Mary Boudreaux, my academic advisor as an undergraduate at LSU who laid out the pathway to graduate school, thank you for always helping me and supporting me on and off the field. Your impact measures much greater than any degree you helped your athletes achieve. To the late Dr. Lisa Bertman, your mentorship and guidance fills my heart every day. God Bless you Lisa. To Dr. William Waters, you took a chance on me and served as a valuable mentor early in my training and I am forever indebted to you for that. To Dr. Phillip J. Brantley, you were my challenger and critiquer all in one. Few serve both roles, but you did. I will never forget a passing conversation with you after presenting my specialty examination that reinforced what it took to be a true professional in this career. I had made a statement that was meant to bypass what you were asking, but you were not accepting it. You challenged me and I stayed up all night researching all 565 answers on the MMPI2 and why my patient had answered the questions and why it was inconsistent with the clinical presentation. The next day, after no sleep, you asked me again while I was giving a formal presentation in front of 30 of my colleagues. I was able to answer the question and you smiled and leaned back in your chair. You then said, "That was all I wanted, for you to find out the answer. I did not worry about what the conclusion was other than you had done your job." I have never forgotten the power of that lesson and I carry it with me today. To Dr. Alan Sirota, thank you for the friendship and professional mentoring. I will never forget the days that you would stick your head up in the little window on the doors of the Providence VA Medical Center and smile at me. To Dr. Justin Nash, thank you for allowing me to be me and continuing to demand that I stay that way. I was not the traditional intern/resident in the Brown program, but instead of dismissing me, you challenged me and inspired me to be better everyday. I hope I am making you proud Justin. Thank you for all you have done for me. To Dr. Lorraine Perkins, thank you for your support early in my pharmaceutical career. To Dr. Kimberly Herriott, thank you for being the impetus for me to start The MindSide and continuing the support today. As you were managing me, I can imagine that there were days that you were laughing and crying in the same breath, but you inspired me and supported me to leave a very comfortable job to follow my dream and you laid out the plan for me to get there. Thank you!

In the sports world as a psychologist, I would like to thank the following who started or continue to impact my career. Thank you to Hank Johnson for giving me my start. Thank you to Wayne Flint for the great conversations. Thank you to Tony Ruggiero for everything and I mean that. Tony, you supported me from the very beginning and continue to do so. I am so proud of your success and continued growth in the golf world, and more great things are coming your way. Thank you cannot express my appreciation to you enough. To Eric Eshleman, thank you for taking a chance on me with a world-class player. To Mark Blackburn, thank you for your professional mentoring, guidance, and most importantly, your friendship. You have never let me rest of the standards of my efforts, and have challenged me to be better in everything I do. You took a chance on me with a young player with all the talent in the world, and through it all, he has done well my friend. You continue to introduce me to the decision makers in the game and do so by asking nothing in return. Thank you.

To John Morr and Anthony Grant formerly of the University of Alabama Basketball team, thank you for bringing me in to help the team. From that search on Google, many great things have happened. To Jeff Allen and Ginger Gilmore Childress of the University of

Acknowledgements

Alabama Sports Medicine and Athletic Department, thank you for trusting me and having the innovative mindset to create a resource for your student-athletes that is world-class! To Patrick Murphy of the University of Alabama Softball team, thank you for your support, interest, and investment to work with your players. More importantly, thank you for the impromptu notes and parking lot conversations. To coaches Dana Duckworth, Jenny Mainz, George Husack, Wes Hart, Mic Potter, Jay Seawell, Dennis Pursley, and the associated trainers and members of the coaching staff, and the members of the administration, thank you for your friendship and support. I greatly value my relationship with the University of Alabama and I am honored to serve your student-athletes. To Scott Cochran, you know where I am from, but more importantly, you know where my heart and soul is now! RollTide coach! Thank you for listening to what I have to offer, but more importantly, thank you for asking me to contribute. To the others in that building, thank you! The top of the mountain has not been reached yet.

As an athlete, I would like to thank the following. It goes without saying, but I want to thank again Coach Skip Bertman. I do not need to say anything in print that I have not said to you in person, but you changed my life in such a positive way and did so in such a way that I can never thank you enough. Thank you to Coaches Ray "Smoke" Laval, the late DeWayne "Beetle" Bailey, Mike Bianco, Dan Canevari, and Rick Smith at LSU Baseball for never giving up on me. To my teammates, thank you. To my old roommate Todd Walker, thank you for handing the ball back to me at Auburn after I had made a tragic throwing error and looking me straight in the eyes and saying "well, you screwed it up, now fix it and get us out of this." I did just that and saved the game, but I am not sure I would have believed my Manifesto if it were not for your reminder. To my youth coaches, John Fred Gourrier, Steve Polozola, and John Talley, thank you.

Finally, to my family. Thank you to my in-laws Lamar and Gloria Stevens and my sister-in-law Brooke Stevens. You guys have been a tremendous rock to support my pursuits and have given me the best partner a man can ever have. Thank you to Anna Stevens Barnett for introducing me to my best friend for life. Thank you to my wife, Missy. You are my business partner, my support, my best friend, and more importantly, my inspiration. I know you do not like public acknowledgements, so I will stop there and simply say "I love you and am honored to have you in my life." To Howard Oakes, words cannot express the role you have in my life and that of my family now. Thank you for your support and love for our family. To my late father, James McCabe, thank you for always supporting me, pushing me, believing in me, and serving as the role model for me. Your generosity to your family is the benchmark for me to do the same for my family. I miss you daily. Last, but definitely not least, to my mom, Mary Jo McCabe, you are my guide in my life, professionally and personally. You never allowed me to feel sorry for myself or overburdened by the worry in my life. With the simple guidance that you could provide to spark a change in my life, thank you. "What's the worst that can happen?" Right mom? You have consistently demonstrated passion, vision, and dealing with adversity with grace and love. Love you!

References

[1] Bandura, A. (1977). Self-efficacy: Toward a unifying theory of behavioral change. *Psychological Review, 84*, 191-215.

[2] Dweck, C. (2006). *Mindset: The new psychology of success.* New York, NY: Random House.

[3] Duckworth, A. (2016). *Grit: The power of passion and perseverance.* New York, NY: Scribner.

[4] Navy Special Warfare Physical Training Guide. (2016, May 13). Retrieved from http://www.sealswcc.com/navy-swcc-naval-special-warfare-physical-training-guide.html

[5] Csikszentmihalyi, M. (2008). *Flow: the psychology of optimal experience.* New York, NY: Harper Collins.

[6] Kotler, S. (2014). *The rise of superman: Decoding the science of ultimate human performance.* New York, NY: New Harvest.

[7] Thompon, A. (2013). *Red bull scientific summit summary report.* Retrieved from https://issuu.com/redbullstratos/docs/red_bull_stratos_summit_report_final_050213

[8] Kittinger, J. & Ryan, C. (2011). *Come up and get me: An autobiography of Colonel Joe Kittinger.* Albuquerque, NM: University of New Mexico Press.

[9] Hunt, R. (2016, January 14). Pro golf synopsis. Retrieved from http://3jack.blogspot.com/2016/01/the-new-2015-pro-golf-synopsis-is-on.html

[10] Kahneman, D. (2013). *Thinking, fast and slow.* New York, NY: Farrar, Straus, and Giroux.

[11] Kahneman, D. (2013). *Thinking, fast and slow*. Page 284. New York: NY, Farrar, Straus, and Giroux.

[12] Pope, D. & Schweitzer, M. (2011). Is Tiger Woods loss averse? Persistent bias in the face of experience, competition, and high stakes. *American Economic Review, 101*, 129-157.

[13] Burke, B. (2013). Crowds on Mount Everest [blog]. Retrieved from http://eightsummits.com/bills-articles/crowds-on-mt-everest/

[14] Nuwar, R. (2015, October 8). *The tragic tale of Mt. Everest's most famous dead body*. Retrieved by http://www.bbc.com/future/story/20151008-the-tragic-story-of-mt-everests-most-famous-dead-body

[15] Firth PG et al. (2008). Mortality on Mount Everest, 1921-2006: descriptive study. *British Medical Journal, 10*, 1136-1142.

[16] Greenberg, J. (2009, September 12). *The man behind the legend*. Retrieved from http://www.espn.com/chicago/columns/story?id=4468210&columnist=greenberg_jon

To learn more about Dr. Bhrett McCabe and The MindSide, visit us at www.themindside.com or contact us via email at contact@themindside.com.

To sign up for more information on *The MindSide Manifesto* or future books to be released by Dr. Bhrett McCabe, please email us at orders@themindside.com.

Follow Dr. McCabe and The MindSide on Facebook, Twitter, and Instagram @themindside.

D r. Bhrett McCabe is a Licensed Clinical Psychologist holding a PhD degree in clinical psychology from Louisiana State University (LSU) with an emphasis in behavioral medicine, and completed his pre-doctoral internship at Brown University in Providence, RI. While an undergraduate at LSU, Dr. McCabe was a 4-year letterman on the baseball team and was a member of 2 National Championship teams, 3 SEC championship teams and 3 College World Series teams.

Dr. McCabe is a practicing Sports & Performance Psychologist who works with numerous athletes from the PGA and LPGA Tours, NFL, NBA, MMA, and serves as the sports and performance psychologist for one of the largest and most successful Division I collegiate athletic departments in the country. Dr. McCabe has published several academic journal articles, presented numerous scientific presentations, as well as provided insight and authored many articles for trade magazines such as GOLF Magazine, Golf World, and ESPNW, among others. Dr. McCabe's professional perspective is a blending of his own experiences as an elite athlete, his academic credentials and training, and his interactions with the world's best athletes, coaches, and leaders.

86704867R00148

Made in the USA
Columbia, SC
06 January 2018